A Man of Destiny
WINSTON S. CHURCHILL

SIR WINSTON CHURCHILL, K.G., O.M., C.H.

A MAN OF DESTINY WINSTON S. CHURCHILL

By the Editors of COUNTRY BEAUTIFUL

Published by Country Beautiful Foundation, Inc., Waukesha, Wisconsin

in association with Encyclopedia Enterprises, Inc., New York

COUNTRY BEAUTIFUL Magazine is published by Country Beautiful Foundation, Inc., 24198 W. Bluemound Rd., Waukesha, Wis., a nonprofit organization dedicated to strengthening and preserving the physical, cultural and moral values of America and other nations of the world. COUNTRY BEAUTIFUL FOUNDATION, INC. Officers and Directors: Charles H. Kellstadt, Carl N. Jacobs, Arthur J. Schmid Jr., Edward C. Ramacher, Michael P. Dineen, Cy Crawford, Wilfred A. Schuster, Robert L. Polley, Kenneth L. Schmitz.

Excerpt from "The Life and Times of Winston Churchill" reproduced by permission of William H. Wise & Co., Inc., © 1946. Excerpt from "Sinews of Peace" by Winston S. Churchill reprinted by permission of the publishers, Houghton Mifflin Company. Excerpts from "Step by Step" and "Great Contemporaries" are reprinted by permission of G. P. Putnam's Sons, © 1939 by Winston S. Churchill. The essay, "Painting as a Pastime" is reprinted from AMID THESE STORMS by Winston S. Churchill (Copyright 1932 Charles Scribner's Sons; renewal copyright © 1960 Winston S. Churchill) by arrangement with Odhams Books, Ltd. and with the permission of Charles Scribner's Sons. Extracts from the following books by Winston S. Churchill are reprinted with the permission of Charles Scribner's Sons and Odhams Books, Ltd.: *Amid These Storms* (Copyright 1932 Charles Scribner's Sons; renewal copyright © 1960 Winston S. Churchill). Published in England as *Thoughts and Adventures. The Aftermath* (Copyright 1929 Charles Scribner's Sons; renewal copyright © 1957 Winston S. Churchill). *Marlborough, His Life and Times* (Copyright 1933, 1934, 1935 Charles Scribner's Sons; renewal copyright © 1961, 1962, 1963 Winston S. Churchill). *My Early Life: A Roving Commission* (Copyright 1930 Charles Scribner's Sons; renewal copyright © 1958 Winston S. Churchill). The World Crisis: (1911-1918) (Copyright 1923 Charles Scribner's Sons; renewal copyright 1951 Winston S. Churchill). *The World Crisis: The Eastern Front* (Copyright 1931 Charles Scribner's Sons; renewal copyright © 1959 Winston S. Churchill).

PICTURE CREDITS: Wide World: frontispiece; 72-73; 84-85; 91; Radio Times Hulton Picture Library: 8; 18 r.; 21; 32; 35; 40; 58; 59; Paul Popper: 15 r.; 57; Illustrated London News: 22-23; Shane Leslie: 26; Daily Mirror Newspaper Ltd., London: 30 r.; Imperial War Museum: 30 l.; 50 (2); 52; Freelance Photographers Guild: 48-49; Keystone Press Agency: 53; Odhams Books Ltd.: 67, 68, 69, 70, 75, 76, 77, 79, 80, 83, 86, 87, 89.

CONTENTS

Churchill (right) in 1889 with his mother, Jenny Jerome, and brother, Jack.

INTRODUCTION

WINSTON CHURCHILL will in the years to come be remembered most of all as the man who was Prime Minister of Britain during the Second World War. But he had made good his foothold in history long before that conflict. For forty years he had been a well-known public figure, a statesman who had held a record number of different Cabinet offices, an author of several massive historical works which were acknowledged as masterpieces, and beyond all this, a vivid and picturesque personality about whom violent controversy raged. He had many admirers, if few followers; and even his bitterest opponents admitted his brilliance, however little they trusted his judgment.

Throughout his political career Churchill was ever an outstanding figure, with a magnetic attraction for the limelight. Failures could never abash, nor setbacks dishearten him. Whether his contemporaries were with him or against him, they could never thrust him aside and leave him out of account. And they were often against him, for during a large part of his public life Churchill inspired more interest than confidence. His very cleverness, allied as it was with an element of dare-devilry and schoolboy recklessness, counted against him, for in quiet, peaceful days those qualities in a statesman are not regarded with much favor by a democracy, certainly not by the British democracy, which is rather suspicious of cleverness in its rulers. Dash and daring are equally unwelcome, for they may land the nation all unawares in some rash adventure or entanglement. Solid ability, sure-footed caution, and matter-of-fact common sense are the political virtues that normally win the nation's confidence. And on Churchill's luggage these are hardly the labels which have chiefly caught the eye of his fellow passengers.

But with the outbreak of the Second World War, Churchill found the proper field for the exercise of his special talents. He came into his own, and through the war years he captured and held the confidence and affectionate loyalty of the mass of the nation to a degree rivalled by few other statesmen in the country's history. In the tense hours of that grim and deadly struggle, when the need was for brilliance of vision and imagination to outplan the enemy, when risk and peril were on every side, and unstinted daring was the only path to victory, the people recognized that Churchill's gifts, however dubious their value for peacetime politics, were admirably suited to the national emergency. His clever and fertile intellect, ever-youthful courage and power of firm, self-confident decision were just the qualities the nation longed to find in its wartime leader. Daring, cleverness and originality were the needs of the hour.

AN INCARNATION OF JOHN BULL

His bulldog face, twinkling eyes, confident, dominating smile; cigar thrust out jauntily between firm lips; a hat looking too small for the broad head it tried to cover; hand uplifted, brandishing a stick or waving two fingers in a "V" for victory sign, came to be a familiar and cheering picture during those years to the whole of Britain, and indeed to the free peoples of two hemispheres. With the addition of side-whiskers and the appropriate costume, he might have stood as an incarnation of the traditional John Bull. Indeed, his stubborn independence of judgment, his warm-heartedness, generosity and deep-rooted patriotism were quite in keeping with the character of that burly symbol in the union-jack waistcoat. He was, perhaps, less true to type in his quickness of wit and speech, but his wartime oratory truly voiced the mind of the British people. The world outside was not mistaken when it saw in him the embodiment of the temper and determination of the nation whose leader and spokesman he was.

Future historians writing the account of the great struggle against the Nazi-Fascist dictators will be compelled to record that Britain was the mainstay of the forces of liberty, and that Churchill was the dominating figure among the democratic leaders in the conflict. America and Russia both threw immense efforts into the fight, but Britain will take the center of the stage because, but for her original defiance and her lonely stand, there might have been no organized and ultimately successful resistance to Hitler, only a collapse of one country after another in face of external attack and internal treachery. Had Britain fallen, and had her industrial potential thereby been added to the Nazi resources, the assault on Russia would have ended differently, and with Europe, Asia and Africa subject to Germany and Italy, America herself would have faced disaster. Civilization owes Winston Churchill a great debt because he not only led and inspired the resistance of Britain, but succeeded in drawing the United Nations together into a strongly woven partnership, and maintained their unity and co-operation throughout the war by his tireless efforts.

DETESTED, CRITICIZED, ATTACKED AND APPLAUDED

At one time or another in his long and varied career Churchill was detested by every political party. He was savagely attacked, criticized, derided by men of responsible judgment. He was approved, admired and applauded on other occasions as wholeheartedly by those very same men.

It may be taken for granted that there was reason behind both verdicts. For all mortal men are faulty and fallible, and the bigger the scale of the man, the more visible are his defects. Gulliver was repelled by the coarse skins of the giants of Brobdingnag, while he marvelled at the smooth complexions of the Lilliput dwarfs. However golden the head of the idol, its feet will be common clay. Churchill was no exception to that rule.

In recent times it has been the fashion for biographers to concentrate on the clay, to exhaust themselves in "debunking" their heroes, stressing their faults and frailties and trying to belittle their greatness. No doubt they get a great satisfaction from this game—for game it is, not honest biography. None but a fool can seriously contend that a man whose capacities and achievements have raised him head and shoulders above his contemporaries is really nothing but a mean little fellow in the bottom class. If great men are not always without blemish as their admirers pretend, if they have the defects of their virtues, they may still be great.

Churchill was a great man. Bonar Law, his bitter critic, was yet compelled to admit: "In mental power and vital force, he is one of the foremost men in the country." He was not by any means always wise or infallible. There were lights and shadows in his character, and we can look frankly at them both, not expecting perfection, but knowing, nevertheless, that when the account is cast, the lights will show a big credit balance over the shadows.

In any review of Churchill's qualities one fact thrusts itself at once to the fore: he was at heart a soldier.

The career of arms was his own first choice; and although the years he actually spent in military service were few, they were crowded with battle experience eagerly sought and whole-heartedly enjoyed. "Don't you like war?" he blithely asked one of his officers as they stood in a trench under heavy bombardment. He had a very full measure of that physical courage which revels in the thrill of danger. In his writings about his experiences, he might confess to moments of fear, but that feeling never seems to have deterred him from taking the wildest risks.

The fact is that Churchill delighted in action; and battle, where action is at its keenest intensity and the stakes are life and death, is of all human occupations the one which gives the richest satisfaction to such a craving. Action was one of the keys to his character. He was not in the accepted sense of the term a thinker. He thought, of course; thought with quite remarkable vigor and clarity. But the aim and object of his thinking was not abstract knowledge but concrete performance. He thought in order to act. Quiet meditation upon the truth behind the face of things did not lure him. His natural bent was not towards matters of mind, and when in his writings he occasionally wandered into some such problem there was an air of childish simplicity about his remarks. As a young man, he found himself once involved in a discussion with some learned friends fresh from Oxford, and was soon swept far out of his depth by their clever reasoning. "I must go to Oxford," he resolved. But he never went. It was not his spiritual home.

ARTIST, ORATOR AND AUTHOR

Churchill was not a philosopher; he was an artist. Mere activity was not enough. It must be a finished performance. Whatever he did —and he was eager always to do anything to which his active hands could be set—was done with technical efficiency and that infinite capacity for taking pains which is proverbially the mark of genius.

He was an artist with his pen. As a man of letters he ranks very high indeed. Though a master of classic elegance, he was never too polished and dignified to be arresting, exciting and hugely entertaining in his books. He produced tales of travel, biography, autobiography, history, and even, in his early days, a novel. The novel is not perhaps in the front rank of its kind; but the high place of his other work is assured.

Above: Westminster Hall rises majestically above the House of Lords in the Parliament building.

Below: Churchill enters an automobile in Sicily during one of many trips to the Mediterranean.

About his performance as an orator there can be no two opinions. Here his desire to excel came up against the crippling handicap of a speaking defect—a kind of lisp that thickened his S's—which might have kept a less determined man off the platform. So well did he overcome that vocal difficulty that his hearers were hardly aware of it, and were swiftly caught up and carried forward on the tide of an eloquence that gripped, delighted and inspired them. His language was direct, vivid, magnificent. He put immense pains into the preparation of these speeches, even of the apparently impromptu jests. He was unequalled as a phrase-maker. He could clothe ideas in words that men remember; quaint and unexpected at times, as in the description of an inaccurate statement as a "terminological inexactitude"; splendid at others, as in his tribute to the airmen heroes of the Battle of Britain: "Never in the field of human conflict was so much owed by so many to so few."

His delight in craftsmanship found many outlets; for he had to ever be making something. His skill as a painter is well known, and landscapes from his brush have found an honored place in the homes of eminent art collectors. For years his easel and canvases went abroad with him on all his holiday travels. In earlier days he frequently piloted his own airplane. He turned his hand to bricklaying, and acquired the art of building a wall well and truly at the correct trade union rate of progress. Some giant intellects are housed in very helpless and unhandy bodies, devoid of practical skill. Their fingers, as the saying runs, are all thumbs. Churchill was not of their number. He had a craftsman's hands and a craftsman's temperament.

PERTINACITY AND PREMONITION

To his tireless industry he added another gift—that of quite extraordinary pertinacity. If Churchill wanted something, he went for it till he got it, and nothing could deter him. When he wanted to join Kitchener's Sudan campaign, he hammered at every door, up to that of the Prime Minister himself, and when none opened, still persisted till he found a back entrance. He trod the earth with the confident step of one who feels himself an owner, not a trespasser, wherever he goes.

One gift he had, which from time to time showed itself uncannily —the power of premonition. It was not always active, and normally he could look ahead only as well as any other knowledgeable and clear-thinking man. But now and again he uttered a prophecy edged with more than ordinary foresight. Shrewd deduction? Lucky guesswork? Maybe. Maybe not. Was there in the complex web of his ancestry some Celtic strain that momentarily and unpredictably sharpened his subconscious mind with the penetration of second sight, as it often tinged his speech with an Irish quality of wit?

Some of these forecasts find mention in the following pages. Another, perhaps less precise but no less heavy with premonition, occurred in February, 1938, at the end of his speech deploring Anthony Eden's departure from the Foreign Office:

> "I predict that the day will come at some point or other, on some issue or other, when you will have to make a stand, and I pray to God that when that day comes we may not find, through an unwise foreign policy, we may have to make that stand alone!"

Two and a quarter years later that warning was fulfilled to the letter.

The widespread distrust which pursued Churchill throughout the greater part of his political career sought its justification in his successive changes of party, his open disagreement with his party leaders,

11

his advocacy at different times of conflicting policies. He labored under the charge of unreliability.

On the face of it, there was good warrant for this charge. Winston started in politics as a Tory—a Tory Democrat of the school founded by his father, Lord Randolph Churchill. He criticized his leaders, quarrelled with them, attacked them and crossed the floor of the House to join their opponents, the Liberals. There for some years he associated with the Radical wing, and supported them in urging a reduction of naval expenditure. Then, at the Admiralty, he became a zealous spender on the Navy and a problem to his former allies. He served as a Coalition Liberal under Lloyd George, but when the Coalition fell, he drifted away from the party and called himself a Constitutionalist, under which title he rejoined the Tories. Later on, however, he challenged his leader, Stanley Baldwin, on the Indian question, and slid into the position of an independent Tory critic of the substantially Tory government.

WHEN CHURCHILL CHANGED SIDES

These changes of side are facts of his history. When they were thrown up at him once in the House, he blandly retorted: "To improve is to change. To be perfect is to have changed often." But the answer was hardly a true explanation of his changes. They were the result, not of some effort of self-improvement, but of fidelity to what he already was. He was most true to himself when most indefinite in his party loyalties. For the fact is that Churchill was not, in the accepted sense, a good party man. He would not swallow and digest the policies thrust on him by any party. Always he had to choose and decide for himself. His party had but one member—Winston Churchill.

If he must wear a label, then that of Tory Democracy suits him best. Born in a ducal palace, with the blue blood of a long aristocratic lineage in his veins, he instinctively inclined towards a benevolently feudal outlook. He had warm human interests, the kindliest goodwill to his fellow citizens, and a healthy confidence in their essential worth. He was ready to be a big brother to them all, so long as they gave the role of leadership to him. He could call himself a Tory. He could call himself a Liberal. He could never call himself a Socialist, for any suggestion of dictatorship by the proletariat was abhorrent to him.

Leadership, however, means service, and to Churchill the notion that those in authority should use their power to pursue personal ends, to feather private nests, while leaving those they govern in poverty, wretchedness or suffering, was no less abhorrent. He broke with the Tories over Tariff Reform, when he saw their big business interests plotting a protectionist racket to exploit the public for the benefit of their own pockets. He left the Liberals when he deemed them to be betraying the country to the Socialists in the hope of saving thereby the remnants of their shattered party. He quarrelled with Baldwin when he thought the Tory leader was letting go the Empire; weakly shirking his responsibilities to the masses of India for the sake of his own tranquility and failing to maintain Britain's tradition of care for her dependent peoples. To himself, Churchill seemed always consistent, however inconsistent his course might appear to others, and however faulty might be the judgment upon which he based his attitude.

His consistency was, however, the practice of uniformly acting according to his nature and his immediate judgment with regard to each particular situation. His reactions to current events were swift and vigorous. He was no crafty plotter or schemer, pursuing long-distance plans and subtle intrigues. His nature was frank, open and

12

Above: Piccadilly Circus, a famed London landmark, is the city's entertainment center.

Below: The National Gallery at Trafalgar Square, named for the British naval victory over France.

ingenuous, and within the limits of honor, kindliness and fair play his course tended to be opportunist. It is natural, therefore, that those who judged him by the standard of their own fixed party loyalties and undeviating plans and purposes should deem him erratic, elusive and unreliable.

DEVOTION TO HIS OWN OPINIONS

It must be admitted that Winston's rather exaggerated devotion to his own personal view of affairs often proved embarrassing and exasperating to those with whom he teamed up. They found him lacking in the team spirit; and it was not, to speak the truth, highly developed in him. John Morley once said of him and Lloyd George: "Whereas Winston knows his own mind, Lloyd George is always more concerned to know the minds of other people." It was a shrewd analysis of the contrast between the two men, and drew attention to that feature in Winston's character which strongly colored the whole of it. Winston was intensely subjective. What he himself was thinking, feeling, planning, experiencing, was all important. What other people thought or experienced was of very little consequence to him, except in so far as it affected his own affairs. No doubt we all tend to look out on life rather in this fashion, but in Churchill the personal view was very pronounced. His natural instinct was always to take the lead. Others were at liberty to follow if they chose.

"The proper study of mankind," said Alexander Pope, "is man." Winston pursued this study upon the man nearest to him—himself— with eager interest and ceaseless curiosity. The curiosity became at times almost detached and impersonal, as for instance when he was knocked down by an auto in New York in 1932, and proceeded to record from his sickbed a detailed account of his exact sensations at the time of the accident, and picturesque calculations of the stresses his body had undergone. This exaggerated interest in his own mental and physical processes and experiences is shown again and again in his writings. It came out in his speeches. It dominated his thought.

Such a quality is of course far more excusable in him than it would be in a lesser man. For after all, Churchill was quite the most lively and gifted and exciting personality that Churchill had ever met or was likely to meet, with a wider range of experience and a more varied assortment of talents than any of his contemporaries. He knew that this was so, and as he was by temperament incapable of false modesty, as he was of any other form of duplicity, he made no pretense of thinking that other people's ideas were as important or well founded as his own.

Although he had a generous and kindly nature, with plenty of goodwill to his neighbors, this self-absorption interfered with the growth of a steady fellowship with them. Pursuing his own ideas and trains of thought, he was suddenly surprised to find that he was out of step with his companions—or they, as he judged, with him—and was rather hurt that they blamed him for the discord. Obviously, it must be their fault, and he was puzzled by their antagonism. "I have never joined in any intrigue," he protested in 1912. "Everything I have got, I have worked for; and I've been more hated than anybody."

AMBITIOUS, WILLFUL AND MISCHIEVOUS

No doubt there was warrant for his complaint, and yet the fault did not altogether lie with his critics. They were excusably annoyed at the young man's undisguised ambition and his air of infallibility. Besides it must be embarrassing for a group of politicians when their colleague takes the bit between his teeth and goes boring along on his own course, heedless of the generally accepted policy. Especially must this be so when that course has been chosen on the spur of the moment, on grounds which are not clear to them or seem inadequate. And Churchill had a natural preference for an original way of his own. When he was going up Vesuvius in 1910, he ignored the beaten track, and insisted on choosing his own more direct route. He nearly broke his neck.

He had yet another characteristic which helps to explain the hostility that pursued him during so much of his career. As a small boy, he was very willful and mischievous, and he never entirely grew up. Still, from time to time, that streak of mischief would come to the surface.

H. G. Wells once wrote: "There are times when the evil spirit comes upon him, and then I can only think of him as an intractable little boy, a mischievous, dangerous little boy, a knee-worthy little boy. Only by thinking of him in that way can I go on liking him." Age never quenched the imp in him. In party controversy he would sometimes startle the public and disconcert his allies by his reckless utterances, or by explosions of childish petulance. And while he enjoyed opposition he could not bear criticism.

We have still to reach that quality in Churchill which warrants us calling him great. For a man may be gifted far above the ordinary, a remarkable figure in his generation, without earning a title to real greatness. For that, he must devote himself to a great cause, use his abilities in a mighty enterprise. Only the man who can lose his life in the service of some noble purpose will save it unto life eternal.

Churchill had brilliant gifts. He was, in addition, driven by a limitless ambition. Without such ambition, men rarely rise to greatness.

> "Fame is the spur that the clear spirit doth raise
> (That last infirmity of noble mind)
> To scorn delights, and live laborious days."

But had Churchill been no more than a clever egoist, concerned merely to outshine his fellows, and grasp all the prizes, he would not have been truly great. He might only have been a disturbing nuisance. A man must have something bigger and finer than himself as the object of his ambition if he is to win enduring fame.

Men are made great by the causes they serve. George Washington was ennobled by his service to the freedom of the American colonies; Lincoln by his fight to free the slaves and establish a united American democracy. Gladstone had a passion for liberty—the liberty of small nations everywhere. Lloyd George was dominated by an instinctive craving to help the underdog. All had great gifts. But it was the purpose to which they used those gifts which stamped their fame on history.

What was Churchill's deepest passion? What in him was stronger than his personal ambition?

He at one time or another used his great abilities on behalf of various causes. Free Trade evoked his first major political efforts, even to the sacrifice of his party loyalties. Later, he devoted himself wholeheartedly to the problem of alleviating the lot of the unemployed. "I would give my life," he once declared, "to see them placed on a right footing in regard to their lives and means of living." But in fact neither of these issues quite gripped the central core of the man. His Free Trade convictions were largely accepted from the economic doctrines of the day. He was not himself an economist. His activities in social reform owed much of their inspiration and most of their content to his close association with Lloyd George, who planned

The late President John F. Kennedy confers honorary United States citizenship on Winston Churchill in April, 1963. Churchill's son, Randolph (right, facing the President), accepted the honor on behalf of his famous father.

the measures which Churchill carried out for Unemployment Insurance. Later on in his career, Churchill acquiesced in a policy of protective tariffs, and showed a much diminished zeal about current unemployment problems.

THE SERVICE OF HIS COUNTRY

It was left for the Second World War to demonstrate and to bring into full prominence that central passion which was bigger in Churchill than any self-seeking ambition, and made him the giant figure which the world admiringly recognizes today. Fighter, reformer, artist, Churchill was above all a patriot, with a flaming and overmastering loyalty to Britain, to her honor, her greatness, her Empire, her destiny. He might hold lightly by party ties. He might abandon and oppose former colleagues. He might forget the old time-honored doctrines and ignore or disavow the policies he once acclaimed. But round one pivot he always swung truly. Bigger than his thirst for fame, his hopes of success and dreams of greatness, was his limitless devotion to the service of his country.

His interest always centered chiefly on Imperial and international affairs. Britain's defense by sea, land and air; her dealings with her Colonial possessions, and with the great Dominions joined with her in the British Commonwealth; her friendship with that other mighty English-speaking democracy, the United States; and her relations with allied or rival Powers; these were throughout his career the matters of first concern to Churchill.

Happy is the man who has found his right place and task. Winston Churchill always felt himself to be destined and fore-ordained to some mission of supreme importance for his country. The many almost miraculous escapes from death which studded his career gave support to that faith. Like General Charles "Chinese" Gordon, he might assert the conviction: "I am immortal till my work is done!" In the fullness of time his hour arrived, and the task for which he had been born.

Britain may well be grateful to the Providence which, at the moment when her need was most desperate, brought forth the man ideally equipped by ability, experience and warlike temper to lead her through her darkest night of peril.

MALCOLM THOMSON

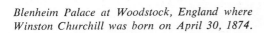

Blenheim Palace at Woodstock, England where Winston Churchill was born on April 30, 1874.

London's Tower Bridge, as it stood during Churchill's boyhood. It provided a closing setting to his long life when his casket passed under the historic structure during the funeral journey down the Thames River.

MY EARLY LIFE
1930

At "The Little Lodge"

IT WAS at "The Little Lodge"[1] I was first menaced with Education. The approach of a sinister figure described as "the Governess" was announced. Her arrival was fixed for a certain day. In order to prepare for this day Mrs. Everest[2] produced a book called *Reading without Tears*. It certainly did not justify its title in my case. I was made aware that before the Governess arrived I must be able to read without tears. We toiled each day. My nurse pointed with a pen at the different letters. I thought it all very tiresome. Our preparations were by no means completed when the fateful hour struck and the Governess was due to arrive. I did what so many oppressed peoples have done in similar circumstances: I took to the woods. I hid in the extensive shrubberies—forests they seemed—which surrounded "The Little Lodge". Hours passed before I was retrieved and handed over to "the Governess". We continued to toil every day, not only at letters but at words, and also at what was much worse, figures. Letters after all had only got to be known, and when they stood together in a certain way one recognized their formation and that it meant a certain sound or word which one uttered when pressed sufficiently. But the figures were tied into all sorts of tangles and did things to one another which it was extremely difficult to forecast with complete accuracy. You had to say what they did each time they were tied up together, and the Governess apparently attached enormous importance to the answer being exact. If it was not right it was wrong. It was not any use being "nearly right". In some cases these figures got into debt with one another: you had to borrow one or carry one, and afterwards you had to pay back the one you had borrowed. These complications cast a steadily gathering shadow over my daily life. They took one away from all the interesting things one wanted to do in the nursery or in the garden. They made increasing inroads upon one's leisure. One could hardly get time to do any of the things one wanted to do. They became a general worry and preoccupation. More especially was this true when we descended into a dismal bog called "sums". There appeared to be no limit to these. When one sum was done, there was always another. Just as soon as I managed to tackle a particular class of these afflictions, some other much more variegated type was thrust upon me.

My mother took no part in these impositions, but she gave me to understand that she approved of them and she sided with the Governess almost always. My picture of her in Ireland is in a riding habit, fitting like a skin and often beautifully spotted with mud. She and my father hunted continually on their large horses; and sometimes there were great scares because one or the other did not

---

[1] The home of Lord Randolph Churchill in Dublin when he acted as Secretary to his father, the Duke of Marlborough, the Viceroy.
[2] His nurse.

In 1893 Churchill entered the Royal Military Academy at Sandhurst. The young cavalry cadet enjoyed his training and began to plan a lifetime career as an army officer.

Churchill as a 15-year-old student at Harrow. Although not a good student, he worked hard to pass his examinations to enter military academy.

come back for many hours after they were expected.

My mother always seemed to me a fairy princess: a radiant being possessed of limitless riches and power. She shone for me like the Evening Star. I loved her dearly—but at a distance.

Gaining a Prize

It was thought incongruous that while I apparently stagnated in the lowest form, I should gain a prize open to the whole school for reciting to the headmaster twelve hundred lines of Macaulay's "Lays of Ancient Rome" without making a single mistake. I also succeeded in passing the preliminary examination for the Army while still almost at the bottom of the school. This examination seemed to have called forth a very special effort on my part, for many boys far above me in the school failed in it. I also had a piece of good luck. We knew that among other questions we should be asked to draw from memory a map of some country or other. The night before by way of final preparation I put the names of all the maps in the atlas into a hat and drew out New Zealand. I applied my good memory to the geography of that Dominion. Sure enough the first question in the paper was: "Draw a map of New Zealand". This was what is called at Monte Carlo an *en plein*, and I ought to have been paid thirty-five times my stake. However, I certainly got paid very high marks for my paper.

Death of His Nurse

[In 1895] Mrs. Everest died. As soon as I heard she was seriously ill I travelled up to London to see her. She lived with her sister's family in North London. She knew she was in danger, but her only anxiety was for me. There had been a heavy shower of rain. My jacket was wet. When she felt it with her hands she was greatly alarmed for fear I should catch cold. The jacket had to be taken off and thoroughly dried before she was calm again. Her only desire was to see my brother Jack, and this unhappily could not be arranged. I set out for London to get a good specialist, and the two doctors consulted together upon the case, which was one of peritonitis. I had to return to Aldershot by the midnight train for a very early morning parade. As soon as it was over, I returned to her bedside. She still knew me, but she gradually became unconscious. Death came very easily to her. She had lived such an innocent and loving life of service to others and held such a simple faith that she had no fears at all, and did not seem to mind very much. She had been my dearest and most intimate friend during the whole of the twenty years I had lived. I now telegraphed to the clergyman with whom she had served nearly a quarter of a century before. He had a long memory for faithful service. We met at the graveside.

When I think of the fate of poor old women, so many of whom have no one to look after them and nothing to live on at the end of their lives, I am glad to have had a hand in all that structure of pensions and insurance which no other country can rival and which is especially a help to them.

The Well-to-Do

When I am in the Socratic mood and planning *my* Republic, I make drastic changes in the education of the sons of well-to-do citizens. When they are sixteen or seventeen they begin to learn a craft and to do healthy manual labour, with plenty of poetry, songs, dancing, drill and gymnastics in their spare time. They can thus let off their steam on something useful. It is only when they are really thirsty for knowledge, longing to hear about things, that I would let them go to the University. It would be a favour, a coveted privilege, only to be given to those who had either proved their worth in factory or field or whose qualities and zeal were pre-eminent. However, this would upset a lot of things; it would cause commotion and bring me perhaps in the end a hemlock draught.

THE STORY OF THE
MALAKAND FIELD FORCE

1898

Army Life

I pause to consider for a moment the conditions, and circumstances, by which the pursuit of a military career differs from all others. In political life, in art, in engineering, the man with talents who behaves with wisdom may steadily improve his position in the world. If he makes no mistakes he will probably achieve success. But the soldier is more dependent upon external influences. The only way he can hope to rise above the others is by risking his life in frequent campaigns. All his fortunes, whatever they may be, all his position and weight in the world, all his accumulated capital, as it were, must be staked afresh each time he goes into action. He may have seen twenty engagements, and be covered with decorations and medals. He may be marked as a rising soldier. And yet each time he comes under fire his chances of being killed are as great as, and perhaps greater than, those of the youngest subaltern, whose luck is fresh. The statesman, who has put his power to the test, and made a great miscalculation, may yet retrieve his fortunes. But the indiscriminating bullet settles everything.

The Wounded

The cheeriness and patience of the wounded men exceeds belief. Perhaps it is due to a realization of the proximity in which they have stood to death; perhaps partly to that feeling of relief, with which a man turns for a spell from war to peace. In any case it is remarkable. A poor fellow—a private in the Buffs—was hit at Zagai, and had his arm amputated at the shoulder. I expressed my sympathy, and he replied, philosophically: "You can't make omelettes without breaking eggs", and after a pause added, with much satisfaction, "The regiment did well that day." He came of a fighting stock, but I could not help speculating on the possible future which awaited him. Discharge from the service as medically unfit, some miserable pension insufficient to command any pleasures but those of drink, a loafer's life, and a pauper's grave. Perhaps the regiment—the officers, that is to say—would succeed in getting him work, and would from their own resources supplement his pension. But what a wretched and discreditable system is that, by which the richest nation in the world neglects the soldiers who have served it well, and which leaves to newspaper philanthropy, to local institutions, and to private charity, a burden which ought to be proudly borne by the State.

A statesman may err,
but for the soldier,
the indiscriminating bullet
settles everything . . .

When 22-years-old, Churchill served with the 4th
Hussars at Bangalore, India as an army officer.

Soldier's Courage

The courage of the soldier is not really contempt for physical evils and indifference to danger. It is a more or less successful attempt to simulate these habits of mind. Most men aspire to be good actors in the play. There are a few who are so perfect that they do not seem to be actors at all. This is the ideal after which the rest are striving. It is one very rarely attained.

Three principal influences combine to assist men in their attempts: preparation, vanity and sentiment. The first includes all the force of discipline and training. The soldier has for years contemplated the possibility of being under fire. He has wondered vaguely what kind of an experience it would be. He has seen many who have gone through it and returned safely. His curiosity is excited. Presently comes the occasion. By road and railway he approaches daily nearer to the scene. His mind becomes familiar with the prospect. His comrades are in the same situation. Habit, behind which force of circumstances is concealed, makes him conform. At length the hour arrives. He observes the darting puffs of smoke in the distance. He listens to the sounds that are in the air. Perhaps he hears something

*Sentiment is the
quality that makes
a soldier a hero ...*

FINAL CHARGE OF THE 21st LANCERS
*In 1898, Churchill was attached to the 21st Lancers and served on the
Nile Expeditionary Force. In the subsequent battle of Omdurman on
the upper reaches of the Nile, Sir Herbert Kitchener broke the power of
the Dervishes and revenged Gordon. Lieutenant Churchill was in the*

strike with a thud and sees a soldier near him collapse like a shot
pheasant. He realizes that it may be his turn next. Fear grips him
by the throat.

Then vanity, the vice which promotes so many virtues, asserts
itself. He looks at his comrades and they at him. So far he has shown
no sign of weakness. He thinks, they are thinking him brave. The
dearly longed-for reputation glitters before his eyes. He executes
the orders he receives.

But something else is needed to make a hero. Some other influence
must help him through the harder trials and more severe ordeals,
which may befall him. It is sentiment which makes the difference
in the end. Those who doubt should stroll to the camp fire one
night and listen to the soldiers' songs. Every one clings to something
that he thinks is high and noble, or that raises him above the rest
of the world in the hour of need. Perhaps he remembers that he is
sprung from an ancient stock, and of a race that has always known
how to die; or more probably it is something smaller and more
intimate; the regiment, whatever it is called—"The Gordons",
"The Buffs", "The Queen's"—and so nursing the name—only the
unofficial name of an infantry battalion after all—he accomplishes
great things and maintains the honour and the Empire of the British
people.

AT THE BATTLE OF OMDURMAN
final cavalry charge which routed the enemy. This contemporary drawing of the action, reproduced by courtesy of the "Illustrated London News," is by Caton Woodville, who lived from 1856 to 1927 and was acknowledged to be one of the most famous military artists of his time.

LONDON TO LADYSMITH

1900

Too Much Surrendering

Two days before, I had written to an officer in high command at home, whose friendship I have the honour to enjoy: "There has been a great deal too much surrendering in this war, and I hope people who do so will not be encouraged." Fate had intervened, yet though her tone was full of irony she seemed to say, as I think Ruskin once said, "It matters very little whether your judgments of people are true or untrue, and very much whether they are kind or unkind," and repeating that I will make an end.

Prisoner of War

The position of a prisoner of war is painful and humiliating. A man tries his best to kill another, and finding that he cannot succeed asks his enemy for mercy. The laws of war demand that this should be accorded, but it is impossible not to feel a sense of humbling obligation to the captor from whose hand we take our lives. All military pride, all independence of spirit must be put aside. These

Left: Churchill was graduated from military academy in 1894 and commissioned an officer in the British Army.

Right: Colorful mounted sentries are part of the British military tradition which included Churchill's service.

may be carried to the grave, but not into captivity. We must prepare ourselves to submit, to obey, to endure. Certain things—sufficient food and water and protection during good behaviour—the victor must supply or be a savage, but beyond these all else is favour. Favours must be accepted from those with whom we have a long and bitter quarrel, from those who feel fiercely that we seek to do them cruel injustice. The dog who has been whipped must be thankful for the bone that is flung to him.

The Dutch Aversion

What is the true and original root of Dutch aversion to British rule? It is not Slagters Nek, nor Broomplatz, nor Majuba, nor the Jameson Raid. Those incidents only fostered its growth. It is the abiding fear and hatred of the movement that seeks to place the native on a level with the white man. British government is associated in the Boer farmer's mind with violent social revolution. Black is to be proclaimed the same as white. The servant is to be raised against the master; the Kaffir is to be declared the brother of the European, to be constituted his legal equal, to be armed with political rights. The dominant race is to be deprived of their superiority; nor is a tigress robbed of her cubs more furious than is the Boer at this prospect.

£ 25.—.—

(vijf en twintig pond stg.) belooning uitgeloofd door de Sub-Commissie van wijk V voor den Specialen Constabel dezer wijk, die den ontvluchte Krijgsgevangene

Churchill

levend of dood te dezer kantore aflevert. —

Namens de Sub- Comm.
wijk V

Lodk de Haas
Sec

Translation.

£25

(Twenty-five Pounds stg.) REWARD is offered by the Sub-Commission of the fifth division, on behalf of the Special Constable of the said division, to anyone who brings the escaped prisioner of war

CHURCHILL,

dead or alive to this office.

For the Sub-Commission of the fifth division.
(Signed) LODK. de HAAS, Sec.

NOTE.-The Original Reward for the arrest of Winston Churchill on his escape from Pretoria, posted on the Government House at Pretoria, brought to England by the Hon. Henry Mashem, and is now the property of W. R. Burton.

IAN HAMILTON'S MARCH

1900

The Gordon Highlanders

A melancholy spectacle broke upon my view. Near a clump of rocks eighteen Gordon Highlanders lay dead in a row. Their faces were covered with blankets, but their grey stockinged feet—for the boots had been removed—looked very pitiful. There they lay stiff and cold on the surface of the great Banket Reef. I knew how much more precious their lives had been to their countrymen than all the gold mines the lying foreigners say this war was fought to win. And yet, in view of the dead and the ground they lay on, neither I nor the officer who rode with me could control an emotion of illogical anger, and we scowled at the tall chimneys of the Rand.

General Ian Hamilton, General Smith-Dorrien, all their staffs, and everyone who wished to pay a last tribute of respect to brave

Colorful highlander pipers parade in London during traditional English military ceremonies.

men, attended the funerals. The veteran regiment stood around the grave, forming three sides of a hollow square—Generals and staff filled the other. The mourning party rested on their arms, reversed; the Chaplain read the Burial Service, the bodies were lowered into the trench, and the pipes began the lament. The wild, barbaric music filled the air, stirring the soldiers, hitherto quite unmoved, with a strange and very apparent force. Sad and mournful was the dirge wailing of battles ended, of friendships broken, and ambitions lost; and yet there were mingled with its sadness many notes of triumph, and through all its mourning rang the cry of hope.

The many notes of triumph; the cry of hope . . .

Red tunics, towering bearskin hats and the ringing commands of an English Guard officer mark age-old military ceremonies.

THE WORLD CRISIS

1911–1918

1931

The curtain falls upon the long front in France and Flanders. The soothing hands of Time and Nature, the swift repair of peaceful industry, have already almost effaced the crater-fields and the battle lines which in a broad belt from the Vosges to the sea lately blackened the smiling fields of France. The ruins are rebuilt, the riven trees are replaced by new plantations. Only the cemeteries, the monuments and stunted steeples, with here and there a mouldering trench or huge mine-crater lake, assail the traveller with the fact that twenty-five millions of soldiers fought here and twelve millions shed their blood or perished in the greatest of all human contentions less than twenty years ago. Merciful oblivion draws its veils; the crippled limp away; the mourners fall back into the sad twilight of memory. New youth is here to claim its rights, and the perennial stream flows forward even in the battle zone, as if the tale were all a dream.

Is this the end? Is it to be merely a chapter in a cruel and senseless story? Will a new generation in their turn be immolated to square the black accounts of Teuton and Gaul? Will our children bleed and gasp again in devastated lands? Or will there spring from the very fires of conflict that reconciliation of the three giant combatants, which would unite their genius and secure to each in safety and freedom a share in rebuilding the glory of Europe?

Top: The Gothic interior of Westminster Abbey.
Below: Big Ben crowns the Houses of Parliament.

THE WORLD CRISIS
THE EASTERN FRONT
1931

The Russian Revolution

Many streams had flowed together to bring the deluge. The Russian revolution was begun by social, military and political forces which within a week were left aghast behind it. In its opening paroxysm all conscious Russia participated. It was primarily a patriotic revolt against the misfortunes and mismanagement of the War. Defeats and disasters, want of food and prohibition of alcohol, the slaughter of millions of men, joined with inefficiency and corruption to produce a state of exasperation among all classes which had no outlet but revolt, could find no scapegoat but the Sovereign. For a year past the Czar and his wife had been the objects of growing universal resentment. The fond, obstinate husband and father, the absolute monarch obviously devoid of all the qualities of a national

BACK INTO THE ARMY

In November, 1915, Churchill was commissioned a Major in t Oxfordshire Yeomanry and in this photograph he is seen in the unifo of this regiment. He was transferred to the Grenadier Guards a later promoted Lieutenant-Colonel in the 6th Royal Scots Fusilie

CHURCHILL VISITS THE SOMME BATTLEFIELD
In this group, taken in 1915, Churchill is standing beside General Emile Fayolle, Commander of the French Sixth and First Armies in the Battle of the Somme. In the following year, Churchill left the Army for good, since his command had disappeared with the amalgamation of the 6th Royal Scots Fusiliers with another battalion.

ruler in times of crisis, bore the burden of all the sufferings which the German Armies had inflicted on the Russian State. Behind him the Empress, a still more hated figure, dwelt in her tiny circle listening only to her cronies—her lady companion Madame Virubova, her spiritual adviser the sensual mystic Rasputin—and presumed thence and on such promptings to sway the whole policy and fortunes of the tormented Empire.

In vain the Imperial family, deeply concerned for their own existence—apart from all other issues—approached their Head. In vain the leaders of the Duma and every independent figure in Russia made their protests. In vain the Ambassadors of the Allied Powers dropped their elaborate hints, or even uttered solemn and formal warnings under the direction of their governments. Nicholas II, distressed, remained immovable. He saw as clearly as they did the increasing peril. He knew of no means by which it could be averted. In his view nothing but autocracy established through centuries had enabled the Russians to proceed thus far in the teeth of calamity. No people had suffered and sacrificed like the Russians. No State, no nation, had ever gone through trials on such a scale

WITH KING GEORGE V AT MILITARY EXERCISES
This photograph of Winston Churchill talking to George V was taken in 1913, the year before the First World War. Churchill had kept closely in touch with Continental military matters and in consequence his judgments about them were well-informed.

*The Russian revolution;
a patriotic revolt
against war...*

Prime Minister Lloyd George (left)
appointed Churchill to his cabinet as
Secretary of State for War and Air.

and retained its coherent structure. The vast machine creaked and
groaned. But it still worked. One more effort and victory would
come. To change the system, to open the gate to intruders, to part
with any portion of the despotic power, was in the eyes of the Czar
to bring about a total collapse. Therefore, though plunged daily
deeper in anxiety and perplexity, he was held alike by all his
instincts and his reasoning faculties in a fixed position. He stood
like a baited animal tied to a stake and feebly at bay.

Change at All Costs

All sorts of Russians made the revolution. No sort of Russian
reaped its profit. Among the crowds who thronged the turbulent
streets and ante-rooms of Petrograd in these March days, with
resolve for "Change at all costs" in their hearts, were found Grand
Dukes, fine ladies, the bitterest die-hards and absolutists like
Purishkevitch and Yusupov; resolute, patriotic politicians like
Rodzianko and Guchkov; experienced Generals; diplomatists and
financiers of the old regime; Liberals and Democrats; Socialists like
Kerensky; sturdy citizens and tradesfolk; faithful soldiers seeking to
free their Prince from bad advisers; ardent nationalists resolved to
purge Russia from secret German influence; multitudes of loyal
peasants and workmen; and behind all, cold, calculating, ruthless,
patient, stirring all, demanding all, awaiting all, the world-wide
organization of International Communism.

ROYAL TANK REGIMENT IN GERMANY
*A leading part in the evolution of the tank was played by Churchill,
and he was also very largely responsible for inspiring the idea of the
armoured car. He is here inspecting some British armoured cars shortly
after the close of the First World War in 1918.*

THE AFTERMATH

1929

Armistice

On the night of the Armistice I dined with the Prime Minister at
Downing Street. We were alone in the large room from whose
walls the portraits of Pitt and Fox, of Nelson and Wellington, and
—perhaps somewhat incongruously—of Washington then looked
down. One of the most admirable traits in Mr. Lloyd George's
character was his complete freedom at the height of his power,
responsibility and good fortune from anything in the nature of
pomposity or superior airs. He was always natural and simple. He
was always exactly the same to those who knew him well: ready to
argue any point, to listen to disagreeable facts even when con-
troversially presented. One could say anything to him, on the terms
that he could say anything back. The magnitude and absolute
character of the victory induced a subdued and detached state of
mind. There was no feeling that the work was done. On the contrary, the realization was strong upon him that a new and perhaps
more difficult phase of effort was before him. My own mood was
divided between anxiety for the future and desire to help the fallen
foe. The conversation ran on the great qualities of the German
people, on the tremendous fight they had made against three-
quarters of the world, on the impossibility of rebuilding Europe
except with their aid. At that time we thought they were actually
starving, and that under the twin pressures of defeat and famine the
Teutonic peoples—already in revolution—might slide into the
grisly gulf that had already devoured Russia.

Lenin

Lenin was also Vengeance. Child of the bureaucracy, by birth a petty noble, reared by a locally much respected Government School Inspector, his early ideas turned by not unusual contradictions through pity to revolt extinguishing pity. Lenin had an unimpeachable father and a rebellious elder brother. This dearly loved companion meddled in assassination. He was hanged in 1894. Lenin was then sixteen. He was at the age to feel. His mind was a remarkable instrument. When its light shone it revealed the whole world, its history, its sorrows, its stupidities, its shams, and above all its wrongs. It revealed all facts in its focus—the most unwelcome, the most inspiring—with an equal ray. The intellect was capacious and in some phases superb. It was capable of universal comprehension in a degree rarely reached among men. The execution of the elder brother deflected this broad white light through a prism: and the prism was red.

But the mind of Lenin was used and driven by a will not less exceptional. The body tough, square and vigorous in spite of disease was well fitted to harbour till middle age these incandescent agencies. Before they burnt it out his work was done, and a thousand years will not forget it. Men's thoughts and systems in these ages are moving forward. The solutions which Lenin adopted for their troubles are already falling behind the requirements and information of our day. Science irresistible leaps off at irrelevant and henceforth dominating tangents. Social life flows through broadening and multiplying channels. The tomb of the most audacious experimentalist might already bear the placard "Out of date". An easier generation lightly turns the pages which record the Russian Terror. Youth momentarily interested asks whether it was before or after the Great War; and turns ardent to a thousand new possibilities. The educated nations are absorbed in practical affairs. Socialists and Populists are fast trooping back from the blind alleys of thought and scrambling out of the pits of action into which the Russians have blundered. But Lenin has left his mark. He has won his place. And in the cutting off of the lives of men and women no Asiatic conqueror, not Tamerlane, not Jenghiz Khan can match his fame.

Implacable vengeance, rising from a frozen pity in a tranquil, sensible, matter-of-fact, good-humoured integument! His weapon logic; his mood opportunist. His sympathies cold and wide as the Arctic Ocean; his hatreds tight as the hangman's noose. His purpose to save the world: his method to blow it up. Absolute principles, but readiness to change them. Apt at once to kill or learn: dooms and afterthoughts: ruffianism and philanthropy. But a good husband; a gentle guest; happy, his biographers assure us, to wash up the dishes or dandle the baby; as mildly amused to stalk a capercailzie as to butcher an Emperor. The quality of Lenin's revenge was impersonal. Confronted with the need of killing any particular person he showed reluctance—even distress. But to blot out a million, to proscribe entire classes, to light the flames of intestine war in every land with the inevitable destruction of the well-being of whole nations—these were sublime abstractions.

Lenin's intellect: a broad white light deflected through a red prism . . .

MR. CHURCHILL IN HIS STUDY AT WESTERHAM

Between 1933 and 1938, Churchill published his masterpiece, "Marlborough," a life of his famous eighteenth-century ancestor, in four large volumes. Meanwhile, in 1937, he had collected a number of personal sketches on "Great Contemporaries," in which he had written anecdotes about a diverse collection of celebrities of all nations.

Lenin was the Grand Repudiator. He repudiated everything. He repudiated God, King, Country, morals, treaties, debts, rents, interest, the laws and customs of centuries, all contracts written or implied, the whole structure—such as it is—of human society. In the end he repudiated himself. He repudiated the Communist system. He confessed its failure in an all-important sphere. He proclaimed the New Economic Policy and recognized private trade. He repudiated what he had slaughtered so many for not believing. They were right it seemed after all. They were unlucky that he did not find it out before. But these things happen sometimes: and how great is the man who acknowledges his mistake! Back again to wash the dishes and give the child a sweetmeat. Thence once more to the rescue of mankind. This time perhaps the shot will be better aimed. It may kill those who are wrong: not those who are right. But after all what are men? If Imperialism had its cannon food, should the Communist laboratory be denied the raw material for sociological experiment?

When the subtle acids he had secreted ate through the physical texture of his brain Lenin mowed the ground. The walls of the Kremlin were not the only witnesses of a strange decay. It was reported that for several months before his death he mumbled old prayers to the deposed gods with ceaseless iteration. If it be true, it shows that Irony is not unknown on Mount Olympus. But this gibbering creature was no longer Lenin. He had already gone. His body lingered for a space to mock the vanished soul. It is still preserved in pickle for the curiosity of the Moscow public and for the consolation of the faithful.

Lenin's intellect failed at the moment when its destructive force was exhausted, and when sovereign remedial functions were its quest. He alone could have led Russia into the enchanted quagmire; he alone could have found the way back to the causeway. He saw;

WITH KING EDWARD VIII

In the constitutional crisis of December, 1936, the King had asked permission to see Churchill as a private friend. Mr. Churchill had been his staunch supporter in the events leading up to the abdication, and he tried to persuade Mr. Baldwin to take no irrevocable step without first giving a formal statement of events before Parliament.

The story of the human race is war...

he turned; he perished. The strong illuminant that guided him was cut off at the moment when he had turned resolutely for home. The Russian people were left floundering in the bog. Their worst misfortune was his birth: their next worst—his death.

War in Our Age

The story of the human race is War. Except for brief and precarious interludes there has never been peace in the world; and before history began murderous strife was universal and unending. But the modern developments surely require severe and active attention.

Up to the present time the means of destruction at the disposal of man have not kept pace with his ferocity. Reciprocal extermination was impossible in the Stone Age. One cannot do much with a clumsy club. Besides, men were so scarce and hid so well that they were hard to find. They fled so fast that they were hard to catch. Human legs could only cover a certain distance each day. With the best will in the world to destroy his species, each man was restricted to a very limited area of activity. It was impossible to make any effective progress on these lines. Meanwhile one had to live and hunt and sleep. So on the balance the life-forces kept a steady lead over the forces of death, and gradually tribes, villages, and governments were evolved.

The effort at destruction then entered upon a new phase. War became a collective enterprise. Roads were made which facilitated the movement of large numbers of men. Armies were organized. Many improvements in the apparatus of slaughter were devised. In particular the use of metal, and above all, steel, for piercing and cutting human flesh, opened out a promising field. Bows and arrows, slings, chariots, horses, and elephants lent a valuable assistance. But here again another set of checks began to operate. The governments were not sufficiently secure. The armies were liable to violent internal disagreements. It was extremely difficult to feed large numbers of men once they were concentrated, and consequently the efficiency of the efforts at destruction became ⁓ful and was tremendously hampered by defective organization. Thus again there was a balance on the credit side of life. The world rolled forward, and human society entered upon a vaster and more complex age.

STEP BY STEP

1936—1939

1939

Avoiding War

The dear desire of all the peoples, not perhaps even excluding a substantial portion of the German people themselves, is to avoid another horrible war in which their lives and homes will be destroyed or ruined and such civilization as we have been able to achieve reduced to primordial pulp and squalor. Never till now were great communities afforded such ample means of measuring their approaching agony. Never have they seemed less capable of taking effective measures to prevent it. Chattering, busy, sporting, toiling, amused from day to day by headlines and from night to night by cinemas, they yet can feel themselves slipping, sinking, rolling backward to the age when "the earth was void and darkness moved upon the face of the waters". Surely it is worth a supreme effort— the laying aside of every impediment, the clear-eyed facing of fundamental facts, the noble acceptance of risks inseparable from heroic endeavour—to control the hideous drift of events and arrest calamity upon the threshold. Stop it! Stop it!! Stop it now!!! NOW is the appointed time.

A Well-Armed America

When things are going well in America, the more solid pedestrian forces in the free countries of Europe are conscious of a new draught of strength. When things go ill, they are weakened through a hundred channels in those very elements of strength which ought to reward law-respecting, peace-interested, civilized States. Economic and financial disorder in the United States not only depresses all sister countries, but weakens them in those very forces which might either mitigate the hatreds of races or provide the means to resist tyranny. The first service which the United States can render to world causes is to be prosperous and well-armed.

The arming part is being achieved on a very large scale. Enormous supplies have been voted by Congress for the expansion of the armed forces, particularly the Navy, to levels far above what any immediate direct danger would seem to require. No American party resists the President's desire to make the United States one of the most heavily armed, scientifically prepared countries in the world. Pacifism and the cult of defencelessness have been discarded by all parties. There never was in peace a time when the American armaments by land, air and sea, reached so imposing a height, or were sustained by so much national conviction.

Reassurance Needed

But above all, I fear a proposal that we should abandon the right to have an Air Force, in Mr. Baldwin's words, at least "equal to that of any Power within striking distance of these shores". I fear the kind of argument which will say, if Germany consents to be only a third as strong as Britain on the seas, is it not reasonable that Britain should consent to be only a half, or a third, or some fraction, of the strength of Germany in the air? To agree to that would be to betray the life and independence of the British nation. All these matters must weigh heavily with us while we are awaiting the results of the Prime Minister's impending negotiations with Herr Hitler. And the government would do well to speak with more plainness upon these issues and give reassurance to the country, in so far as they are in a position to do so.　　　[17 November, 1938]

Hitler's Mind

One can understand very readily how Hitler's mind has worked. He regarded Munich as an act of submission on the part of Britain and France under the threat of war. No one knew better than he the inherent weakness of his own position at that time. His generals and financial experts had warned him of the risks he ran. He felt that he knew the limits of the will-power of those against whom he was matched. He was sure that the sincere love of peace which inspired the British and French governments would lead them to give way under pressure. He ascribed their action when they did so only to the basest motives. All their conscientious scruples about self-determination for the Sudeten-Germans were to him only the evidences of their lack of fighting quality. When what he had predicted to his circle was confirmed by the event, his confidence in his instinct and in his star bounded high.

If the Nazi Dictator had the time to study English history he would see that on more than one famous occasion this island had lost great military advantages in Europe by its intense reluctance to be involved in Continental struggles, and has yet in the end led the way to victory. He had only to read the last two years of the reign of King William III and the opening years of Queen Anne to learn that an improvident unwillingness to enter a quarrel may be succeeded by unwearying and triumphant leadership in that same quarrel at a later date and more difficult stage. How could Louis XIV believe that the England which had tamely watched his occupation of all the Belgian fortresses in 1701 would reach a long arm to strangle his armies on the Danube in 1704?

LORD RANDOLPH CHURCHILL

1906

IN AUGUST of 1873 Lord Randolph went to Cowes upon what proved to him a memorable visit. In honour of the arrival of the Czarewich and the Czarevna the officers of the cruiser *Ariadne*, then lying as guard-ship in the Roads, gave a ball, to which all the pleasure seekers who frequent the Solent at this season of the year made haste to go in boats and launches from the shore and from the pleasure fleet. Here for the first time he met Miss Jerome, an American girl whose singular beauty and gifted vivacity had excited general attention. He was presented to her by a common friend. Waltzing made him giddy, and he detested dancing of all kinds; so that after a formal quadrille they sat and talked. She was living with her mother and eldest sister at Rosetta Cottage, a small house which they had taken for the summer, with a tiny garden facing the sea. Thither the next night, duly bidden, he repaired to dine. The dinner was good, the company gay and attractive, and with the two young ladies chatting and playing duets at the piano the evening passed very pleasantly. She was nineteen, and he scarcely twenty-four; and, if Montaigne is to be believed, this period of extreme youth is Love's golden moment. That very night Miss Jerome told her laughing and incredulous sister of a presentiment that their new friend was the man she would marry; and Lord Randolph confided to Colonel Edgecumbe, who was of the party, that he admired the two sisters and meant, if he could, to make "the dark one" his wife.

Next day they met again "by accident"—so runs the account I have received—and went for a walk. That evening he was once more a guest at Rosetta Cottage. That night—the third of their acquaintance—was a beautiful night, warm and still, with the lights of the yachts shining on the water and the sky bright with stars. After dinner they found themselves alone in the garden, and—brief courtship notwithstanding—he proposed and was accepted.

So far as the principals were concerned, everything was thus

LORD RANDOLPH AT WORK

After an early career of great promise, ill-health curtailed the political activities of Lord Randolph Churchill, Winston's father. His last term of office as Chancellor of the Exchequer ended in 1886. Although in Parliament until his death in 1895 at the age of 46, he was in the end a chronic invalid. He is shown above, preparing a speech.

easily and swiftly settled, and the matter having become so earnest all further meetings were suspended until the Duke of Marlborough and Mr. Jerome, who was in America, had been consulted. Lord Randolph returned to Blenheim shaken by alternating emotions of joy and despondency. He had never been in love before and the force and volume of the tide swept him altogether off his feet. At one moment he could scarcely believe that one so unworthy as he could have been preferred; the next he trembled lest all his hopes should be shattered by circumstances unforeseen. Nor indeed was his anxiety without reason; for many and serious obstacles had yet to be encountered and smoothed away.

*My father knew
his mind
in many things . . .*

The Duke was very seriously disturbed at the news of his son's intention and declined to commit himself to any expression of approval until he had made searching inquiry into the standing and circumstances of the Jerome family. He deplored the precipitancy with which the decision had been taken. "It is not likely," he wrote upon 31 August, "that at present you can look at anything except from your own point of view; but persons from the outside cannot but be struck with the unwisdom of your proceedings, and the uncontrolled state of your feelings, which completely paralyses your judgment." His rebuke was supported by his wife, who urged affectionate counsels of caution, patience and self-restraint, and was pointed by a set of witty and satirical verses from his brother, Lord Blandford, setting forth the unhappy fate of those who marry in haste and repent at leisure.

It will easily be understood how this attitude—most Americans being proud as the devil—raised corresponding objections on the other side. Mr. Jerome was himself in many ways a remarkable personality. He had made and lost and made again considerable fortunes in the enterprise and struggle of American life. He had founded the first two great American racecourses, Jerome Park and Coney Island Jockey Club, and divides with Mr. August Belmont the claim to be the father of the American Turf. He owned and edited the *New York Times*. A vehement Federalist in the Civil War, he was said to have subscribed nearly half his fortune to the Federal war funds. When in 1862 the war party in New York was discredited by the disasters of the campaign, and riotous mobs attacked the *Times* office, Mr. Jerome—having purchased a battery of cannon and armed his staff with rifles—beat them off, not without bloodshed. Altogether he was a man of force and versatility. He had at first, indeed, written a conditional assent to his daughter's engagement, but he withdrew it with promptness as soon as he heard a murmur of opposition. Mrs. Jerome and her daughters retreated to France; and all interviews, and even communications, were forbidden by all the parents. Randolph Churchill, however, knew his own mind in many things, and most especially in this. Such was his vehemence that the Duke was soon persuaded, for the sake of his son's peace of mind and of his own authority, to acquiesce —at any rate, provisionally—in a formal engagement. But he insisted upon delay. Nothing, he declared, but time could prove an affection so rapidly excited; and with this decision, supported and emphasized by the Jeromes, the lovers had perforce to be content.

The parents on both sides only wished to be assured that the attachment of their children was no passing caprice, but a sincere and profound affection; and as the weeks grew into months this conviction was irresistibly borne in upon them. In October the Duke was willing to admit that the period of probation might be considerably curtailed. But he still had strong reasons for not wishing the marriage to take place immediately. The dissolution was certainly in the air. By-election after by-election had gone against Mr. Gladstone's Government. Greenwich, Stroud, Dover, Hull, Exeter, East Staffordshire and Renfrewshire had renounced their allegiance; Bath had been barely retained, and the Solicitor-General, whose victory at Taunton had been a much-paraded compensation,

He was of the
temper that gallops
'til it fails . . .

was threatened with a petition for bribery. It was most important that Woodstock should be held for the Conservatives. No one could possibly have so good a chance as the young cadet born and bred on the soil, who knew half the farmers and local magnates personally, whose excursions with the harriers had made him familiar with all parts of the constituency and whose gay and stormy attractiveness had won him a host of sworn allies.

He had often in words and in letters expressed a disinclination for public life. It is curious to notice how even in the days of buoyant unconquered youth, moods of depression cast their shadows across his path. Although possessed of unusual nervous energy, his whole life was a struggle against ill health. Excitement fretted him cruelly. He smoked cigarettes "till his tongue was sore" to soothe himself. Capable upon emergency of prolonged and vehement exertion, of manifold activities and pugnacities, of leaps and heaves beyond the common strength of men, he suffered by reaction fits of utter exhaustion and despondency. Most people grow tired before they are over-tired. But Lord Randolph Churchill was of the temper that gallops till it falls. An instinct warned him of the perils which threatened him in a life of effort. He shrank from it in apprehension. Peace and quiet, sport and friends, agricultural interests—above all a home—offered a woodland path far more alluring than the dusty road to London. The Duke felt, and with reason, that unless Lord Randolph were member for Woodstock before his marriage, not only would the borough be seduced to Radicalism, but that the son in whom all the hopes and ambitions of his later life were centred might never enter Parliament at all.

Lord Randolph was very grateful for the friendly attitude his family had now assumed and was quite prepared to repay concession by patience in one direction and by energy in another.

The Woodstock election being out of the way, the road was cleared for more important matters. The Duke, his political anxieties laid to rest, journeyed to Paris, saw the young lady for himself, and, returning completely converted, withdrew all remaining stipulations for delay. But further difficulties presented themselves. The question of settlements proved delicate and thorny. Mr. Jerome had strong and, it would seem, not unreasonable views, suggested by American usage, about married women's property and made some propositions which Lord Randolph considered derogatory to him. Although he was to benefit considerably under the arrangement proposed, he refused utterly to agree to any settlement which contained even technical provisions to which he objected; and after an embarrassing discussion went off to prepare determined plans to earn a living "in England or out of it", as fortune should dictate, for himself and his future wife—"a course in which," so he wrote to his father, "I am bound to say she thoroughly agrees with me."

Face to face with this ultimatum—the first of any importance and not the least successful in Lord Randolph's forceful career—Mr. Jerome, who after all only wished to make a proper and prudent arrangement, capitulated after twenty-four hours' consideration. A satisfactory treaty was ratified, and it only remained to fulfil the conditions. The negotiations had already extended over seven months and the ceremony was appointed without further delay. The Duke, though unable to be present himself, sent his blessing in a most cordial letter. "Although, my dear Randolph, you have acted in this business with less than usual deliberation, you have adhered to your choice with unwavering constancy and I cannot doubt the truth and force of your affection." On 15 April, 1874, the marriage was celebrated at the British Embassy in Paris, and after a tour—not too prolonged—upon the Continent, Lord Randolph Churchill returned in triumph with his bride to receive the dutiful laudations of the borough of Woodstock and enjoy the leafy glories of Blenheim in the spring.

MARLBOROUGH
HIS LIFE AND TIMES
1933

The span of mortals is short, the end universal; and the tinge of melancholy which accompanies decline and retirement is in itself an anodyne. It is foolish to waste lamentations upon the closing phase of human life. Noble spirits yield themselves willingly to the successively falling shades which carry them to a better world or to oblivion. Of course, it is more becoming for a warrior to die in battle on the field, in command, with great causes in dispute and strong action surging round; like Charles XII at Frederikshald, like Berwick at Philippsburg, or Wolfe on the Heights of Abraham, or Nelson at Trafalgar. But these swift exits are not in human choice. Great captains must take their chance with the rest. Caesar was assassinated by his dearest friend. Hannibal was cut off by poison. Frederick the Great lingered out years of loneliness in body and soul. Napoleon rotted at St. Helena. Compared with these, Marlborough had a good and fair end to his life.

Early in June, 1722, at Windsor Lodge, he was attacked with further paroxysms, and though his reason was unclouded, his strength began to fail rapidly. He was aware that his end was near.

He lay quietly or in a coma for some hours, and died with the dawn of 16 June in the seventy-third year of his age.

His funeral was a scene of solemn splendour and martial pomp. Sarah would not accept the offers of the State, wishing to bear the expense herself; but the nobility, the Army, and the College of Heralds surrounded and followed the funeral car as it made its way through immense crowds to Westminster Abbey. Eight Dukes, Knights of the Garter, followed the Duke of Montagu, chief mourner, and in the procession walked Cadogan, now Commander-in-Chief, and a group of generals who had shared equally in Marlborough's glories and misfortunes. The coffin was lowered into the vault at the east end of Henry VII's Chapel, and rested there for some years.

Marlborough's death stirred his old soldiers wherever they might be.

GREAT CONTEMPORARIES
1937

GEORGE BERNARD SHAW

Mr. Bernard Shaw was one of my earliest antipathies. Indeed, almost my first literary effusion, written when I was serving as a subaltern in India in 1897 (it never saw the light of day), was a ferocious onslaught upon him, and upon an article which he had written disparaging and deriding the British Army in some minor war. Four or five years passed before I made his acquaintance. My mother, always in agreeable contact with artistic and dramatic circles, took me to luncheon with him. I was instantly attracted by the sparkle and gaiety of his conversation, and impressed by his eating only fruit and vegetables, and drinking only water. I rallied him on the latter habit, asking: "Do you really never drink any wine at all?" "I am hard enough to keep in order as it is," he replied. Perhaps he had heard of my youthful prejudice against him.

Few people practise what they preach, and no one less so than Mr. Bernard Shaw. Few are more capable of having the best of everything both ways. His spiritual home is no doubt in Russia; his native land is the Irish Free State; but he lives in comfortable England. His dissolvent theories of life and society have been sturdily banished from his personal conduct and his home. No one has ever led a more respectable life or been a stronger seceder from his own subversive imagination. He derides the marriage vow and even at times the sentiment of love itself; yet no one is more happily or wisely married. He indulges in all the liberties of an irresponsible Chatterbox, babbling gloriously from dawn to dusk, and at the same time advocates the abolition of Parliamentary institutions and the setting up of an Iron Dictatorship, of which he would probably be the first victim. It is another case for John Morley's comment upon Carlyle, "the Gospel of silence in thirty volumes by Mr. Wordy". He prattles agreeably with the tame English Socialists, and preens himself with evident satisfaction in the smiles alike of Stalin or Mussolini. He promulgates in stern decree that all incomes should be equalized and that anyone who has more than another is guilty—unconsciously perhaps—of personal meanness, if not fraud; he has always preached the ownership of all forms of wealth by the State; yet when the Lloyd George Budget imposed for the first time the slender beginnings of the super-tax, no one made a louder squawk than this already wealthy Fabian. He is at once an acquisitive capitalist and a sincere Communist. He makes his characters talk blithely about killing men for the sake of an idea; but would take great trouble not to hurt a fly.

He seems to derive equal pleasure from all these contrary habits, poses and attitudes. He has laughed his sparkling way through life, exploding by his own acts or words every argument he has ever used on either side of any question, teasing and bewildering every public he has addressed, and involving in his own mockery every cause he has ever championed. The world has long watched with tolerance and amusement the nimble antics and gyrations of this unique and double-headed chameleon, while all the time the creature was eager to be taken seriously.

Hindenburg! The name itself is massive. It harmonizes with the tall thick-set personage with beetling brows, strong features, and heavy jowl, familiar to the modern world. It is a face that you could magnify tenfold, a hundredfold, a thousandfold, and it would gain in dignity, nay, even in majesty; a face most impressive when gigantic. In 1916 the Germans made a wooden image of him, colossal, towering above mankind; and faithful admirers, by scores of thousands, paid their coins to the War Loan for the privilege of hammering a nail into the giant who stood for Germany against the world. In the agony of defeat the image was broken up for firewood. But the effect remained—a giant: slow-thinking, slow-moving but sure, steady, faithful, war-like yet benignant, larger than the ordinary run of men.

He loved the old world of Prussia. He lived in the famous tradition of Frederick the Great. "*Toujours en vedette*", as the German military saying goes—"Always on the look-out." He revelled in the "good old Prussian spirit of Potsdam"; the officer class, poor, frugal, but pursuing honour with feudal fidelity, their whole existence devoted to King and country; a class most respectful to the aristocracy and the lawfully constituted authorities; a class, the enemy of change. Hindenburg had nothing to learn from modern science and civilization except its weapons; no rule of life but duty; no ambition but the greatness of the Fatherland.

THOUGHTS AND ADVENTURES

1932

CONSISTENCY IN POLITICS

A distinction should be drawn at the outset between two kinds of political inconsistency. First, a statesman in contact with the moving current of events and anxious to keep the ship on an even keel and steer a steady course may lean all his weight now on one side and now on the other. His arguments in each case when contrasted can be shown to be not only very different in character, but contradictory in spirit and opposite in direction: yet his object will throughout have remained the same. His resolves, his wishes, his outlook may have been unchanged; his methods may be verbally irreconcilable. We cannot call this inconsistency. In fact it may be claimed to be the truest consistency. The only way a man can remain consistent amid changing circumstances is to change with them while preserving the same dominating purpose. It is inevitable that frequent changes should take place in the region of action. A policy is pursued up to a certain point; it becomes evident at last that it can be carried no further. New facts arise which clearly render it obsolete; new difficulties, which make it impracticable. A new and possibly the opposite solution presents itself with over-

Statesmen must coerce and conciliate...

whelming force. To abandon the old policy is often necessarily to adopt the new. It sometimes happens that the same men, the same government, the same party have to execute this *volte face*. It may be their duty to do so because it is the sole manner of discharging their responsibilities, or because they are the only combination strong enough to do what is needed in the new circumstances. In such a case the inconsistency is not merely verbal, but actual, and ought to be boldly avowed. In place of arguments for coercion, there must be arguments for conciliation; and these must come from the same lips as the former. But all this may be capable of reasonable and honourable explanation. Statesmen may say bluntly, "We have failed to coerce; we have now to conciliate," or alternatively, "We have failed to conciliate; we have now to coerce."

Apart from action in the march of events, there is an inconsistency arising from a change of mood or heart. "*Le cœur a ses raisons que la raison ne connaît pas.*" Few men avoid such changes in their lives, and few public men have been able to conceal them. Usually youth is for freedom and reform, maturity for judicious compromise, and old age for stability and repose. The normal progression is from Left to Right, and often from extreme Left to extreme Right. Mr. Gladstone's progress was by a striking exception in the opposite direction. In the immense period covered by his life he moved steadily and irresistibly from being "the rising hope of stern unbending Tories" to become the greatest Liberal statesman of the nineteenth century. Enormous was the change of mood which this august transition represented. From the young Member of Parliament whose speech against the abolition of slavery attracted the attention of the House of Commons in 1833, from the famous Minister who supported the Confederate States against the North in the sixties, to the fiery orator who pleaded the cause of Bulgarian independence in the eighties, and the veteran Premier, the last scraps of whose matchless strength were freely offered in the nineties to the cause of Irish self-government—it was a transit almost astronomical in its scale.

Change of Party

A change of Party is usually considered a much more serious breach of consistency than a change of view. In fact as long as a man works with a Party he will rarely find himself accused of inconsistency, no matter how widely his opinions at one time on any subject can be shown to have altered. Yet Parties are subject to changes and inconsistencies not less glaring than those of individuals. How should it be otherwise in the fierce swirl of Parliamentary conflict and Electoral fortune? Change with a Party, however inconsistent, is at least defended by the power of numbers. To remain constant when a Party changes is to excite invidious challenge. Moreover, a separation from Party affects all manner of personal relations and sunders old comradeship. Still, a sincere conviction, in harmony with the needs of the time and upon a great issue, will be found to override all other factors; and it is right and in the public interest that it should. Politics is a generous profession. The motives and characters of public men, though constantly criticized, are in the end broadly and fairly judged.

SPEECHES

THE CHOICE FOR EUROPE

FROM AN ADDRESS GIVEN IN THE FREE TRADE HALL,
MANCHESTER, 9 MAY, 1938

But we are told that we must not involve ourselves in a quarrel about ideologies. If this means that we are not to back Communism against Nazism or vice versa, we all agree. Both doctrines are equally obnoxious to the principles of freedom. Certainly we should not back one against the other. But surely we must have an opinion between Right and Wrong? Surely we must have an opinion between Aggressor and Victim? This is no question of resisting Dictators because they are Dictators, but only if they attack other people. Have we not an ideology—if we must use this ugly word— of our own in freedom, in a liberal constitution, in democratic and Parliamentary government, in Magna Carta and the Petition of Right? Ought we not to be ready to make as many sacrifices and exertions for our own broad central theme and cause, as the fanatics of either of these new creeds? Ought we not to produce in defence of Right, champions as bold, missionaries as eager, and, if need be, swords as sharp as are at the disposal of the leaders of totalitarian states?

THE MUNICH AGREEMENT

FROM A SPEECH DELIVERED IN THE HOUSE OF COMMONS
5 OCTOBER, 1938

All is over. Silent, mournful, abandoned, broken, Czechoslovakia recedes into the darkness. She has suffered in every respect by her association with the Western democracies and with the League of Nations, of which she has always been an obedient servant. She has suffered in particular from her association with France, under whose guidance and policy she has been actuated for so long. The very measures taken by His Majesty's Government in the Anglo-French Agreement to give her the best chance possible, namely, the 50 per cent clean cut in certain districts instead of a plebiscite, have turned to her detriment, because there is to be a plebiscite too in wide areas, and those other Powers who had claims have also come down upon the helpless victim. Those municipal elections upon whose voting the basis is taken for the 50 per cent cut were held on issues which had nothing to do with joining Germany. When I saw Herr Henlein over here he assured me that was not the desire of his people.

Positive statements were made that it was only a question of home rule, of having a position of their own in the Czechoslovakian State. No one has a right to say that the plebiscite which is to be taken in areas under Saar conditions, and the clean-cut of the 50 per

cent areas—that those two operations together amount in the slightest degree to a verdict of self-determination. It is a fraud and a farce to invoke that name.

We in this country, as in other Liberal and democratic countries, have a perfect right to exalt the principle of self-determination, but it comes ill out of the mouths of those in totalitarian states who deny even the smallest element of toleration to every section and creed within their bounds. But, however you put it, this particular block of land, this mass of human beings to be handed over, has never expressed the desire to go into the Nazi rule. I do not believe that even now, if their opinion could be asked, they would exercise such an opinion.

When I think of the fair hopes of a long peace which still lay before Europe at the beginning of 1933 when Herr Hitler first obtained power, and of all the opportunities of arresting the growth of the Nazi power which have been thrown away, when I think of the immense combinations and resources which have been neglected or squandered, I cannot believe that a parallel exists in the whole course of history. So far as this country is concerned the responsibility must rest with those who have had the undisputed control of our political affairs. They neither prevented Germany from rearming, nor did they rearm ourselves in time. They quarrelled with Italy without saving Ethiopia. They exploited and discredited the vast institution of the League of Nations and they neglected to make alliances and combinations which might have repaired previous errors, and thus they left us in the hour of trial without adequate national defence or effective international security.

What I find unendurable is the sense of our country falling into the power, into the orbit and influence of Nazi Germany, and of

For more than a decade after World War II, Churchill continued to provide memorable phrases in his many speeches. In Ottawa, Canada, in 1952 (above), he said the free world sought peace but would "withold no sacrifice . . . grudge no toil . . . fear no foe."

our existence becoming dependent upon their good will or pleasure. It is to prevent that, that I have tried my best to urge the maintenance of every bulwark of defence—first, the timely creation of an Air Force superior to anything within striking distance of our shores; secondly, the gathering together of the collective strength of many nations; and thirdly, the making of alliances and military conventions, all within the Covenant, in order to gather together forces at any rate to restrain the onward movement of this power. It has all been in vain. Every position has been successively undermined and abandoned on specious and plausible excuses.

We do not want to be led upon the high road to becoming a satellite of the German Nazi system of European domination. In a very few years, perhaps in a very few months, we shall be confronted with demands with which we shall no doubt be invited to comply. Those demands may affect the surrender of territory or the surrender of liberty. I foresee and foretell that the policy of submission will carry with it restrictions upon the freedom of speech and debate in Parliament, on public platforms, and discussions in the press, for it will be said—indeed, I hear it said sometimes now—that we cannot allow the Nazi system of dictatorship to be criticized by ordinary, common English politicians. Then, with a press under control, in part direct but more potently indirect, with every organ of public opinion doped and chloroformed into acquiescence, we shall be conducted along further stages of our journey.

In 1940, Churchill (above, right) inspects a British coastal defense installation as a key member of the government's Committee of Defense.

A characteristic moment shows Churchill holding a machine gun at a British army post in 1940.

WAR
A SPEECH DELIVERED TO THE HOUSE OF COMMONS
3 SEPTEMBER, 1939

We must not underrate the gravity of the task which lies before us or the temerity of the ordeal, to which we shall not be found unequal. We must expect many disappointments, and many unpleasant surprises, but we may be sure that the task which we have freely accepted is one not beyond the compass and the strength of the British Empire and the French Republic. The Prime Minister said it was a sad day, and that is indeed true, but at the present time there is another note which may be present, and that is a feeling of thankfulness that, if these great trials were to come upon our Island, there is a generation of Britons here now ready to prove itself not unworthy of the days of yore and not unworthy of those great men, the fathers of our land, who laid the foundations of our laws and shaped the greatness of our country.

This is not a question of fighting for Danzig or fighting for Poland. We are fighting to save the whole world from the pestilence of Nazi tyranny and in defence of all that is most sacred to man. This is no war of domination or imperial aggrandisement or material gain; no war to shut any country out of its sunlight and means of progress. It is a war, viewed in its inherent quality, to establish, on impregnable rocks, the rights of the individual, and it is a war to establish and revive the stature of man. Perhaps it might seem a paradox that a war undertaken in the name of liberty and right should require, as a necessary part of its processes, the surrender for the time being of so many of the dearly valued liberties and rights. In these last few days the House of Commons has been voting dozens of Bills which hand over to the executive our most dearly valued traditional liberties. We are sure that these liberties will be in hands which will not abuse them, which will use them for no class or party interests, which will cherish and guard them, and we look forward to the day, surely and confidently we look forward to the day, when our liberties and rights will be restored to us, and when we shall be able to share them with the peoples to whom such blessings are unknown.

THE FIRST MONTH OF WAR
AN ADDRESS BROADCAST 1 OCTOBER, 1939

I do not underrate what lies before us, but I must say this: I cannot doubt we have the strength to carry a good cause forward, and to break down the barriers which stand between the wage-earning masses of every land and that free and more abundant daily life which science is ready to afford. That is my conviction, and I look back upon the history of the past to find many sources of encouragement. Of all the wars that men have fought in their hard pilgrimage, none was more noble than the great Civil War in America nearly eighty years ago. Both sides fought with high conviction, and the war was long and hard. All the heroism of the South could not redeem their cause from the stain of slavery, just as all the courage and skill which the Germans always show in war will not free them from the reproach of Nazism, with its intolerance and its brutality. We may take good heart from what happened in America in those famous days of the nineteenth century. We may be sure that the world will roll forward into broader destinies. We may remember the words of old John Bright after the American Civil War was over, when he said to an audience of English working folk: "At last after the smoke of the battlefield had cleared away, the horrid shape which had cast its shadow over the whole continent had vanished and was gone for ever."

A TIME TO DARE AND ENDURE
FROM AN ADDRESS GIVEN IN THE FREE TRADE HALL, MANCHESTER, 27 JANUARY, 1940

This was no war planned and entered upon by a government, or a class, or a party. On the contrary, the government laboured for peace to the very end; and during those last days the only fear in Britain was lest, weighted down by their awful responsibilities, they should fail to rise up to the height of the occasion. They did not fail, and the Prime Minister led us forward in one great body into a struggle against aggression and oppression, against wrong-doing, faithlessness and cruelty, from which there can be no turning back. We cannot tell what the course of that struggle will be, into what regions it will carry us, how long it will last, or who will fall by the way. But we are sure that in the end right will win, that freedom will not be trampled down, that a truer progress will open, and a broader justice will reign. And we are determined to play our part worthily, faithfully, and to the end.

Come then: let us to the task, to the battle, to the toil—each to our part, each to our station. Fill the armies, rule the air, pour out the munitions, strangle the U-boats, sweep the mines, plough the land, build the ships, guard the streets, succour the wounded, uplift the downcast, and honour the brave. Let us go forward together in all parts of the Empire, in all parts of the island. There is not a week, nor a day, nor an hour to lose.

PRIME MINISTER
A SPEECH DELIVERED IN THE HOUSE OF COMMONS
13 MAY, 1940

On Friday evening last I received His Majesty's Commission to form a new Administration. It was the evident wish and will of Parliament and the nation that this should be conceived on the broadest possible basis and that it should include all parties, both those who supported the late government and also the parties of the Opposition. I have completed the most important part of this task. A War Cabinet has been formed of five Members, representing, with the Opposition Liberals, the unity of the nation. The three party Leaders have agreed to serve, either in the War Cabinet or in high executive office. The three Fighting Services have been filled. It was necessary that this should be done in one single day, on account of the extreme urgency and rigour of events. A number

Freedom will not be trampled down...

of other key positions were filled yesterday, and I am submitting a further list to His Majesty tonight. I hope to complete the appointment of the principal Ministers during tomorrow. The appointment of the other Ministers usually takes a little longer, but I trust that, when Parliament meets again, this part of my task will be completed, and that the administration will be complete in all respects.

To form an Administration of this scale and complexity is a serious undertaking in itself, but it must be remembered that we are in the preliminary stage of one of the greatest battles in history, that we are in action at many points in Norway and in Holland, that we have to be prepared in the Mediterranean, that the air battle is continuous and that many preparations have to be made here at home. In this crisis I hope I may be pardoned if I do not address the House at any length today. I hope that any of my friends and colleagues, or former colleagues, who are affected by the political reconstruction, will make all allowance for any lack of ceremony with which it has been necessary to act. I would say to the House, as I said to those who have joined this government: "I have nothing to offer but blood, toil, tears and sweat."

We have before us an ordeal of the most grievous kind. We have before us many, many long months of struggle and of suffering. You ask, what is our policy? I will say: it is to wage war, by sea, land and air, with all our might and with all the strength that God can give us: to wage war against a monstrous tyranny, never surpassed in the dark, lamentable catalogue of human crime. That is our policy. You ask, what is our aim? I can answer in one word: Victory—victory at all costs, victory in spite of all terror, victory, however long and hard the road may be; for without victory, there is no survival. Let that be realized; no survival for the British Empire; no survival for all that the British Empire has stood for, no survival for the urge and impulse of the ages, that mankind will move forward towards its goal. But I take up my task with buoyancy and hope. I feel sure that our cause will not be suffered to fail among men. At this time I feel entitled to claim the aid of all, and I say, "Come, then, let us go forward together with our united strength."

"BE YE MEN OF VALOUR"
AN ADDRESS BROADCAST 19 MAY, 1940

Having received His Majesty's commission, I have formed an administration of men and women of every party and of almost every point of view. We have differed and quarrelled in the past; but now one bond unites us all—to wage war until victory is won, and never to surrender ourselves to servitude and shame, whatever the cost and the agony may be. This is one of the most awe-striking periods in the long history of France and Britain. It is also beyond doubt the most sublime. Side by side, unaided except by their kith and kin in the great Dominions and by the wide Empires which rest beneath their shield—side by side, the British and French peoples have advanced to rescue not only Europe but mankind from the foulest and most soul-destroying tyranny which has ever darkened and stained the pages of history. Behind them—behind us

Churchill maintained his early interest in military aviation. During a flight across the Atlantic Ocean he was photographed in the cockpit of the Royal Air Force flying boat "Berwick."

—behind the armies and fleets of Britain and France—gather a group of shattered States and bludgeoned races: the Czechs, the Poles, the Norwegians, the Danes, the Dutch, the Belgians—upon all of whom the long night of barbarism will descend, unbroken even by a star of hope, unless we conquer, as conquer we must; as conquer we shall.

Today is Trinity Sunday. Centuries ago words were written to be a call and a spur to the faithful servants of Truth and Justice: "Arm yourselves, and be ye men of valour, and be in readiness for the conflict; for it is better for us to perish in battle than to look upon the outrage of our nation and our altar. As the Will of God is in Heaven, even so let it be."

DUNKIRK

FROM A SPEECH DELIVERED IN THE HOUSE OF COMMONS
4 JUNE, 1940

Turning once again, and this time more generally, to the question of invasion, I would observe that there has never been a period in all these long centuries of which we boast when an absolute guarantee against invasion, still less against serious raids, could have been given to our people. In the days of Napoleon the same wind which would have carried his transports across the Channel might have driven away the blockading fleet. There was always the chance, and it is

Together let us go forward with united strength…

Churchill gives his famous "V" for victory sign which became a symbol of Allied determination during the darkest hours of the Second World War.

that chance which has excited and befooled the imaginations of many Continental tyrants. Many are the tales that are told. We are assured that novel methods will be adopted, and when we see the originality of malice, the ingenuity of aggression, which our enemy displays, we may certainly prepare ourselves for every kind of novel strategem and every kind of brutal and treacherous manoeuvre. I think that no idea is so outlandish, that it should not be considered and viewed with a searching, but at the same time, I hope, with a steady eye. We must never forget the solid assurances of sea-power and those which belong to air power if it can be locally exercised.

I have, myself, full confidence that if all do their duty, if nothing is neglected, and if the best arrangements are made, as they are being made, we shall prove ourselves once again able to defend our island home, to ride out the storm of war, and to outlive the menace of tyranny, if necessary for years, if necessary alone. At any rate, that is what we are going to try to do. That is the resolve of His Majesty's Government—every man of them. That is the will of Parliament and the nation. The British Empire and the French Republic, linked together in their cause and in their need, will defend to the death their native soil, aiding each other like good comrades to the utmost of their strength. Even though large tracts of Europe and many old and famous states have fallen or may fall into the grip of the Gestapo and all the odious apparatus of Nazi rule, we shall not flag or fail. We shall go on to the end, we shall fight in France, we shall fight on the seas and oceans, we shall fight with growing confidence and growing strength in the air, we shall defend our island, whatever the cost may be, we shall fight on the beaches, we shall fight on the landing grounds, we shall fight in the fields and in the streets, we shall fight in the hills; we shall never surrender, and even if, which I do not for a moment believe, this island or a large part of it were subjugated and starving, then our Empire beyond the seas, armed and guarded by the British Fleet, would carry on the struggle, until, in God's good time, the new world, with all its power and might, steps forth to the rescue and the liberation of the old.

A MESSAGE TO THE PEOPLE
BROADCAST 17 JUNE, 1940

The news from France is very bad and I grieve for the gallant French people who have fallen into this terrible misfortune. Nothing will alter our feelings towards them or our faith that the genius of France will rise again. What has happened in France makes no difference to our actions and purpose. We have become the sole champions now in arms to defend the world cause. We shall do our best to be worthy of this high honour. We shall defend our island home and with the British Empire we shall fight on unconquerable until the curse of Hitler is lifted from the brows of mankind. We are sure that in the end all will come right.

THEIR FINEST HOUR
FROM A SPEECH DELIVERED FIRST TO THE HOUSE OF COMMONS AND THEN BROADCAST, 18 JUNE, 1940

What General Weygand called the Battle of France is over. I expect that the battle of Britain is about to begin. Upon this battle depends the survival of Christian civilization. Upon it depends our own British life, and the long continuity of our institutions and our Empire. The whole fury and might of the enemy must very soon be turned on us. Hitler knows that he will have to break us in this island or lose the war. If we can stand up to him, all Europe may be free and the life of the world may move forward into broad, sunlit uplands. But if we fail, then the whole world, including the United States, including all that we have known and cared for, will sink into the abyss of a new Dark Age made more sinister, and perhaps more protracted, by the lights of perverted science. Let us therefore brace ourselves to our duties, and so bear ourselves that, if the British Empire and its Commonwealth last for a thousand years, men will still say, "This was their finest hour."

THE WAR SITUATION
FROM A SPEECH DELIVERED TO THE HOUSE OF COMMONS 20 AUGUST, 1940

The great air battle which has been in progress over this island for the last few weeks has recently attained a high intensity. It is too soon to attempt to assign limits either to its scale or to its duration. We must certainly expect that greater efforts will be made by the enemy than any he has so far put forth. Hostile airfields are still being developed in France and the Low Countries, and the movement of squadrons and material for attacking us is still proceeding. It is quite plain that Herr Hitler could not admit defeat in his air attack on Great Britain without sustaining most serious injury. If, after all his boastings and blood-curdling threats and lurid accounts trumpeted round the world of the damage he has inflicted, of the vast numbers of our Air Force he has shot down, so he says, with so little loss to himself; if after tales of the panic-stricken British crushed in their holes cursing the plutocratic Parliament which has led them to such a plight; if after all this his whole air onslaught were forced after a while tamely to peter out, the Fuhrer's reputation for veracity of statement might be seriously impugned. We may be sure, therefore, that he will continue as long as he has the strength to do so, and as long as any preoccupations he may have in respect of the Russian Air Force allow him to do so.

The enemy is, of course, far more numerous than we are. But our new production already, as I am advised, largely exceeds his, and the American production is only just beginning to flow in. It is a fact, as I see from my daily returns, that our bomber and fighter strengths now, after all this fighting, are larger than they have ever been. We believe that we shall be able to continue the air struggle indefinitely and as long as the enemy pleases, and the longer it continues the more rapid will be our approach, first towards that parity, and then into that superiority in the air, upon which in a large measure the decision of the war depends.

The gratitude of every home in our island, in our Empire, and indeed throughout the world, except in the abodes of the guilty, goes out to the British airmen who, undaunted by odds, unwearied in their constant challenge and mortal danger, are turning the tide of the world war by their prowess and by their devotion. Never in the field of human conflict was so much owed by so many to so few.

TO THE FRENCH PEOPLE
AN ADDRESS BROADCAST TO FRANCE IN FRENCH AND ENGLISH, 21 OCTOBER, 1940

Frenchmen—re-arm your spirits before it is too late. Remember how Napoleon said before one of his battles: "These same Prussians who are so boastful today were three to one at Jena, and six to one at Montmirail." Never will I believe that the soul of France is dead. Never will I believe that her place amongst the greatest nations of the world has been lost for ever! All these schemes and crimes of Herr Hitler's are bringing upon him and upon all who belong to his system a retribution which many of us will live to see. The story is not yet finished, but it will not be so long. We are on his track, and so are our friends across the Atlantic Ocean, and your friends across the Atlantic Ocean. If he cannot destroy us, we will surely destroy him and all his gang, and all their works. Therefore, have hope and faith, for all will come right.

Now what is it we British ask of you in this present hard and bitter time? What we ask at this moment in our struggle to win the victory which we will share with you, is that if you cannot help us, at least you will not hinder us. Presently you will be able to weight the arm that strikes for you, and you ought to do so. But even now we believe that Frenchmen wherever they may be feel their hearts warm and a proud blood tingle in their veins when we have some success in the air or on the sea, or presently—for that will come—upon the land.

Remember we shall never stop, never weary, and never give in, and that our whole people and Empire have vowed themselves to the task of cleansing Europe from the Nazi pestilence and saving the world from the new Dark Ages. Do not imagine, as the German-controlled wireless tells you, that we English seek to take your ships and colonies. We seek to beat the life and soul out of Hitler and Hitlerism. That alone, that all the time, that to the end. We do not covet anything from any nation except their respect. Those Frenchmen who are in the French Empire, and those who are in so-called unoccupied France, may see their way from time to time to useful action. I will not go into details. Hostile ears are listening. As for those, to whom English hearts go out in full, because they see them under the sharp discipline, oppression, and spying of the Hun—as to those Frenchmen in the occupied regions, to them I say, when they think of the future let them remember the words which Gambetta, that great Frenchman, uttered after 1870 about the future of France and what was to come: "Think of it always: speak of it never."

Have hope and faith, for all will come right...

Good night then, sleep to gather strength for the morning. For the morning will come. Brightly will it shine on the brave and true, kindly upon all who suffer for the cause, glorious upon the tombs of heroes. Thus will shine the dawn. *Vive la France!* Long live also the forward march of the common people in all the lands towards their just and true inheritance, and towards the broader and fuller age.

"GIVE US THE TOOLS AND WE WILL FINISH THE JOB"
FROM A BROADCAST ADDRESS, 9 FEBRUARY, 1941

I have been so very careful, since I have been Prime Minister, not to encourage false hopes or prophesy smooth and easy things, and yet the tale that I have to tell today is one which must justly and rightly give us cause for deep thankfulness, and also, I think, for strong comfort and even rejoicing. But now I must dwell upon the more serious, darker and more dangerous aspects of the vast scene of the war. We must all of us have been asking ourselves: what has that wicked man whose crime-stained regime and system are at bay and in the toils—what has he been preparing during these winter months? What new devilry is he planning? What new small country will he overrun or strike down? What fresh form of assault will he make upon our island home and fortress; which—let there be no mistake about it—is all that stands between him and the dominion of the world?

But after all, the fate of this war is going to be settled by what happens on the oceans, in the air, and—above all—in this island. It seems now to be certain that the government and people of the United States intend to supply us with all that is necessary for victory. In the last war the United States sent two million men across the Atlantic. But this is not a war of vast armies, firing immense masses of shells at one another. We do not need the gallant armies which are forming throughout the American Union. We do not need them this year, nor next year; nor any year that I can foresee. But we do need most urgently an immense and continuous supply of war materials and technical apparatus of all kinds. We need them here and we need to bring them here. We shall need a great mass of shipping in 1942, far more than we can build ourselves, if we are to maintain and augment our war effort in the West and in the East.

These facts are, of course, all well known to the enemy, and we must therefore expect that Herr Hitler will do his utmost to prey upon our shipping and to reduce the volume of American supplies entering these islands. Having conquered France and Norway, his clutching fingers reach out on both sides of us into the ocean. I have never underrated this danger, and you know I have never concealed it from you. Therefore, I hope you will believe me when I say that I have complete confidence in the Royal Navy, aided by the Air Force of the Coastal Command, and that in one way or another I am sure they will be able to meet every changing phase of this truly mortal struggle, and that sustained by the courage of our merchant seamen, and of the dockers and workmen of all our ports, we shall outwit, outmanoeuvre, outfight and outlast the worst that the enemy's malice and ingenuity can contrive.

Churchill led the Conservative Party to victory in 1951 and became Britain's Prime Minister for the second time.

In order to win the war Hitler must destroy Great Britain. He may carry havoc into the Balkan States; he may tear great provinces out of Russia; he may march to the Caspian; he may march to the gates of India. All this will avail him nothing. It may spread his curse more widely throughout Europe and Asia, but it will not avert his doom. With every month that passes the many proud and once happy countries he is now holding down by brute force and vile intrigue are learning to hate the Prussian yoke and the Nazi name as nothing has ever been hated so fiercely and so widely among men before. And all the time, masters of the sea and air, the British Empire—nay, in a certain sense, the whole English-speaking world—will be on his track, bearing with them the swords of justice.

The other day, President Roosevelt gave his opponent in the late Presidential Election a letter of introduction to me, and in it he wrote out a verse, in his own handwriting, from Longfellow, which he said, "applies to you people as it does to us". Here is the verse:

> . . . Sail on, O Ship of State!
> Sail on, O Union, strong and great!
> Humanity with all its fears,
> With all the hopes of future years,
> Is hanging breathless on thy fate!

What is the answer that I shall give, in your name, to this great man, the thrice-chosen head of a nation of 130 millions? Here is the answer which I will give to President Roosevelt: Put your confidence in us. Give us your faith and your blessing, and, under Providence, all will be well.

We shall not fail or falter; we shall not weaken or tire. Neither the sudden shock of battle, nor the long-drawn trials of vigilance and exertion will wear us down. Give us the tools, and we will finish the job.

A NEW MAGNA CARTA

A STATEMENT TO THE HOUSE OF COMMONS ON THE PASSING OF THE UNITED STATES "LEASE-AND-LEND" BILL 12 MARCH, 1941

It will not be by German hands that the structure of Europe will be rebuilt or the union of the European family achieved. In every country into which the German armies and the Nazi police have broken there has sprung up from the soil a hatred of the German name and a contempt for the Nazi creed which the passage of hundreds of years will not efface from human memory. We cannot yet see how deliverance will come, or when it will come, but nothing is more certain than that every trace of Hitler's footsteps, every stain of his infected and corroding fingers will be sponged and purged and, if need be, blasted from the surface of the earth.

Hitler may turn and trample this way and that through tortured Europe. He may spread his course far and wide, and carry his curse with him: he may break into Africa or into Asia. But it is here, in this island fortress, that he will have to reckon in the end. We shall strive to resist by land and sea. We shall be on his track wherever

At Dover, England, in 1946 Churchill appeared in the uniform of Lord Warden of the Cinque Ports.

he goes. Our air power will continue to teach the German homeland that war is not all loot and triumph.

We shall aid and stir the people of every conquered country to resistance and revolt. We shall break up and derange every effort which Hitler makes to systematize and consolidate his subjugation. He will find no peace, no rest, no halting-place, no parley. And if, driven to desperate hazards, he attempts the invasion of the British Isles, as well he may, we shall not flinch from the supreme trial. With the help of God, of which we must all feel daily conscious, we shall continue steadfast in faith and duty till our task is done.

This, then, is the message which we send forth today to all the States and nations bond or free, to all the men in all the lands who care for freedom's cause, to our allies and well-wishers in Europe, to our American friends and helpers drawing ever closer in their might across the ocean: this is the message—Lift up your hearts. All will come right. Out of the depths of sorrow and sacrifice will be born again the glory of mankind.

"THE END OF THE BEGINNING"

FROM A SPEECH AT THE LORD-MAYOR'S DAY LUNCHEON AT THE MANSION HOUSE, LONDON, 10 NOVEMBER, 1942

At this time our thoughts turn towards France, groaning in bondage under the German heel. Many ask themselves the question: Is France finished? Is that long and famous history, adorned by so many manifestations of genius and valour, bearing with it so much that is precious to culture and civilization, and above all to the liberties of mankind—is all that now to sink for ever into the ocean of the past, or will France rise again and resume her rightful place in the structure of what may one day be again the family of Europe? I declare to you here, on this considerable occasion, even now when misguided or suborned Frenchmen are firing upon their rescuers, I declare to you my faith that France will rise again. While there are men like General de Gaulle and all those who follow him—and they are legion throughout France—and men like General Giraud, that gallant warrior whom no prison can hold, while there are men like those to stand forward in the name and in the cause of France, my confidence in the future of France is sure.

For ourselves we have no wish but to see France free and strong, with her Empire gathered round her and with Alsace-Lorraine restored. We covet no French possession; we have no acquisitive appetites or ambitions in North Africa or any other part of the world. We have not entered this war for profit or expansion, but only for honour and to do our duty in defending the right.

Let me, however, make this clear, in case there should be any mistake about it in any quarter. We mean to hold our own. I have not become the King's First Minister in order to preside over the liquidation of the British Empire. For that task, if ever it were prescribed, someone else would have to be found, and, under democracy, I suppose the nation would have to be consulted. I am proud to be a member of that vast commonwealth and society of nations and communities gathered in and around the ancient British monarchy, without which the good cause might well have perished from the face of the earth. Here we are, and here we stand, a veritable rock of salvation in this drifting world.

The Churchills greet Queen Elizabeth II at 10 Downing Street In 1955 when Churchill was Prime Minister.

THE DESERT ARMY

A SPEECH TO THE MEN OF THE EIGHTH ARMY AT TRIPOLI
3 FEBRUARY, 1943

It must have been a tremendous experience driving forward day after day over this desert which it has taken me this morning more than six hours to fly at two hundred miles an hour. You were pursuing a broken enemy, dragging on behind you this ever-lengthening line of communications, carrying the whole art of desert warfare to perfection. In the words of the old hymn, you have "nightly pitched your moving tents a day's march nearer home". Yes, not only in the march of the army but in the progress of the war you have brought home nearer. I am here to thank you on behalf of His Majesty's Government of the British Isles and of all our friends the world over.

The days of your victories are by no means at an end, and with forces which march from different quarters we may hope to achieve the final destruction or expulsion from the shores of Africa of every armed German or Italian. You must have felt relief when, after those many a hundred miles of desert, you came once more into a green land with trees and grass, and I do not think you will lose that advantage. As you go forward on further missions that will fall to your lot, you will fight in countries which will present undoubtedly serious tactical difficulties, but which none the less will not have that grim character of desert war which you have known how to endure and how to overcome.

Let me then assure you, soldiers and airmen, that your fellow-countrymen regard your joint work with admiration and gratitude, and that after the war when a man is asked what he did it will be quite sufficient for him to say, "I marched and fought with the Desert Army." And when history is written and all the facts are known, your feats will gleam and glow and will be a source of song and story long after we who are gathered here have passed away.

A SPEECH TO WESTMINSTER COLLEGE, FULTON,
MISSOURI, 5 MARCH, 1946

The safety of the world requires a new unity in Europe, from which no nation should be permanently outcast. It is from the quarrels of the strong parent races in Europe that the world wars we have witnessed, or which occurred in former times, have sprung. Twice in our own lifetime we have seen the United States, against their wishes and their traditions, against arguments, the force of which it is impossible not to comprehend, drawn by irresistible forces into these wars in time to secure the victory of the good cause, but only after frightful slaughter and devastation had occurred. Twice the United States has had to send several millions of its young men across the Atlantic to find the war; but now war can find any nation, wherever it may dwell between dusk and

dawn. Surely we should work with conscious purpose for a grand pacification of Europe, within the structure of the United Nations and in accordance with its Charter. That I feel is an open cause of policy of very great importance.

In front of the iron curtain which lies across Europe are other causes for anxiety. In Italy the Communist Party is seriously hampered by having to support the Communist-trained Marshal Tito's claims to former Italian territory at the head of the Adriatic. Nevertheless the future of Italy hangs in the balance. Again one cannot imagine a regenerated Europe without a strong France. All my public life I have worked for a strong France and I never lost faith in her destiny, even in the darkest hours. I will not lose faith now. However, in a great number of countries, far from the Russian frontiers and throughout the world, Communist fifth columns are established and work in complete unity and absolute obedience to the directions they receive from the Communist centre. Except in the British Commonwealth and in the United States where Communism is in its infancy, the Communist parties or fifth columns constitute a growing challenge and peril to Christian civilization. These are sombre facts for anyone to have to recite on the morrow of a victory gained by so much splendid comradeship in arms and in the cause of freedom and democracy; but we should be most unwise not to face them squarely while time remains.

I repulse the idea that a new war is inevitable; still more that it is imminent. It is because I am sure that our fortunes are still in our own hands and that we hold the power to save the future, that I feel the duty to speak out now that I have the occasion and the opportunity to do so. I do not believe that Soviet Russia desires war. What they desire is the fruits of war and the indefinite expansion of their power and doctrines. But what we have to consider here today while time remains is the permanent prevention of war and the establishment of conditions of freedom and democracy as rapidly as possible in all countries. Our difficulties and dangers will not be removed by closing our eyes to them. They will not be removed by mere waiting to see what happens; nor will they be removed by a policy of appeasement. What is needed is a settlement, and the longer this is delayed, the more difficult it will be and the greater our dangers will become.

Last time I saw it all coming and cried aloud to my own fellow-countrymen and to the world, but no one paid any attention. Up till the year 1933 or even 1935, Germany might have been saved from the awful fate which has overtaken her and we might all have been spared the miseries Hitler let loose upon mankind. There never was a war in all history easier to prevent by timely action than the one which has just desolated such great areas of the globe. It could have been prevented in my belief without the firing of a single shot, and Germany might be powerful, prosperous and honoured today; but no one would listen and one by one we were all sucked into the awful whirlpool. We surely must not let that happen again. This can only be achieved by reaching now, in 1946, a good understanding on all points with Russia under the general authority of the United Nations Organization and by the maintenance of that good understanding through many peaceful years, by the world instrument, supported by the whole strength of the

St. Aldermanbury Church, bombed out during the raids on London during World War II has been reconstructed at Westminster College in Missouri as the Winston Churchill Library.

English-speaking world and all its connexions. There is the solution which I respectfully offer to you in this Address to which I have given the title "The Sinews of Peace".

"A DEEP AND SOLEMN NOTE"

FROM A BROADCAST ADDRESS ON THE DEATH OF
H.M. KING GEORGE VI, 7 FEBRUARY, 1952

My friends, when the death of the King was announced to us yesterday morning there struck a deep and solemn note in our lives which, as it resounded far and wide, stilled the clatter and traffic of twentieth-century life in many lands, and made countless millions of human beings pause and look around them. A new sense of values for the time being took possession of human minds and mortal existence presented itself to so many at the same moment in its serenity and its sorrow, in its splendour and in its pain, in its fortitude and in its suffering.

The King was greatly loved by all his peoples. He was respected as a man and as a prince far beyond the many realms over which he reigned. The simple dignity of his life, his manly virtues, his sense of duty—alike as a ruler and a servant of the vast spheres and communities for which he bore responsibility—his gay charm and happy nature, his example as a husband and a father in his own family circle, his courage in peace or war—all these were aspects of his character which won the glint of admiration, now here, now there, from the innumerable eyes whose gaze falls upon the Throne.

He was sustained not only by his natural buoyancy but by the sincerity of his Christian faith. During these last months the King walked with death as if death were a companion, an acquaintance whom he recognized and did not fear. In the end death came as a friend, and, after a happy day of sunshine and sport, and after "Good night" to those who loved him best, he fell asleep as every man or woman who strives to fear God and nothing else in the world may hope to do.

Queen Elizabeth the Second, like her predecessor, did not pass her childhood in any certain expectation of the Crown. But already we know how well, and we understand why, her gifts and those of her husband, the Duke of Edinburgh, have stirred the only part of our Commonwealth she has yet been able to visit. She has already been acclaimed as Queen of Canada.

We make our claim, and others will come forward too, and tomorrow the proclamation of her sovereignty will command the loyalty of her native land and of all other parts of the British Commonwealth and Empire. I, whose youth was passed in the august, unchallenged, and tranquil glories of the Victorian era, may well feel a thrill in invoking once more the prayer and the anthem, "God save the Queen".

PAINTING AS A PASTIME

An Essay by Winston S. Churchill and A Selection of His Paintings

MANY remedies are suggested for the avoidance of worry and mental overstrain by persons who, over prolonged periods, have to bear exceptional responsibilities and discharge duties upon a very large scale. Some advise exercise, and others, repose. Some counsel travel, and others, retreat. Some praise solitude, and others, gaiety. No doubt all these may play their part according to the individual temperament. But the element which is constant and common in all of them is Change.

Change is the master key. A man can wear out a particular part of his mind by continually using it and tiring it, just in the same way as he can wear out the elbows of his coat. There is, however, this difference between the living cells of the brain and inanimate articles: one cannot mend the frayed elbows of a coat by rubbing the sleeves or shoulders; but the tired parts of the mind can be rested and strengthened, not merely by rest, but by using other parts. It is not enough merely to switch off the lights which play upon the main and ordinary field of interest; a new field of interest must be illuminated. It is no use saying to the tired 'mental muscles' — if one may coin such an expression —'I will give you a good rest,' 'I will go for a long walk,' or 'I will lie down and think of nothing.' The mind keeps busy just the same. If it has been weighing and measuring, it goes on weighing and measuring. If it has been worrying, it goes on worrying. It is only when new cells are called into activity, when new stars become the lords of the ascendant, that relief, repose, refreshment are afforded.

A gifted American psychologist has said, 'Worry is a spasm of the emotion; the mind catches hold of something and will not let it go.' It is useless to argue with the mind in this condition. The stronger the will, the more futile the task. One can only gently insinuate something else into its convulsive grasp. And if this something else is rightly chosen, if it is really attended by the illumination of another field of interest, gradually, and often quite swiftly, the old undue grip relaxes and the process of recuperation and repair begins.

The cultivation of a hobby and new forms of interest is therefore a policy of first importance to a public man. But this is not a business that can be undertaken in a day or swiftly improvised by a mere command of the will. The growth of alternative mental interests is a long process. The seeds must be carefully chosen; they must fall on good ground; they must be sedulously tended, if the vivifying fruits are to be at hand when needed.

To be really happy and really safe, one ought to have at least two or three hobbies, and they must all be real. It is no use starting late in life to say: 'I will take an interest in this or that.' Such an attempt only aggravates the strain of mental effort. A man may acquire great knowledge of topics unconnected with his daily work, and yet hardly get any benefit or relief. It is no use doing what you like; you have got to like what you do. Broadly speaking, human beings may be divided into three classes; those who are toiled to death, those who are worried to death, and those who are bored to death. It is no use offering the manual labourer, tired out with a hard week's sweat and effort, the chance of playing a game of football or baseball on Saturday afternoon. It is no use inviting the politician or the professional or business man, who has been working or worrying about serious things for six days, to work or worry about trifling things at the week-end.

As for the unfortunate people who can command everything they want, who can gratify every caprice and lay their hands on almost every object of desire—for them a new pleasure, a new excitement is only an additional satiation. In vain they rush frantically round from place to place, trying to escape from avenging boredom by mere clatter and motion. For them discipline in one form or another is the most hopeful path.

It may also be said that rational, industrious, useful human beings are divided into two classes: first, those whose work is work and whose pleasure is pleasure; and secondly, those whose work and pleasure are one. Of these the former are the majority. They have their compensations. The long hours in the office or the factory bring with them as their reward, not only the means of sustenance, but a keen appetite for pleasure even in its simplest and most modest forms. But Fortune's favoured children belong to the second class. Their life is a natural harmony. For them the working hours are never long enough. Each day is a holiday, and ordinary holidays when they come are grudged as enforced interruptions in an absorbing vocation. Yet to both classes the need of an alternative outlook, of a change of atmosphere, of a diversion of effort, is essential. Indeed, it may well be that those whose work is their pleasure are those who most need the means of banishing it at intervals from their minds.

The most common form of diversion is reading. In that vast and varied field millions find their mental comfort. Nothing makes a man more reverent than a library. 'A few books,' which was Lord Morley's definition of anything under five thousand, may give a sense of comfort and even of complacency. But a day in a library, even of modest dimensions, quickly dispels these illusory sensations. As you browse about, taking down book after book from the shelves and contemplating the vast, infinitely varied store of knowledge and wisdom which the human race has accumulated and preserved, pride, even in its most innocent forms, is chased from the heart by feelings of awe not untinged with sadness. As one surveys the mighty array of sages, saints, historians, scientists, poets and philosophers whose treasures one will never be able to admire—still less enjoy—the brief tenure of our existence here dominates mind and spirit.

Think of all the wonderful tales that have been told, and well told, which you will never know. Think of all the searching inquiries into matters of great consequence which you will never pursue. Think of all the delighting or disturbing ideas that you will never share. Think of the mighty labours which have been accomplished for your service, but of which you will never reap the harvest. But from this melancholy there also comes a calm. The bitter sweets of a pious despair melt into an agreeable sense of compulsory resignation from which we turn with renewed zest to the lighter vanities of life.

'What shall I do with all my books?' was the question; and the answer, 'Read them,' sobered the questioner. But if you cannot read them, at any rate handle them and, as it were, fondle them. Peer into them. Let them fall open where they will. Read on from the first sentence that arrests the eye. Then turn to another. Make a voyage of discovery, taking soundings of uncharted seas. Set them back on their shelves with your own hands. Arrange them on your own plan, so that if you do not know what is in them, you at least know where they are. If they cannot be

Churchill wrote that painting provided his "diversion of effort" which he believed essential to persons whose hobbies could not be mere extensions of their work.

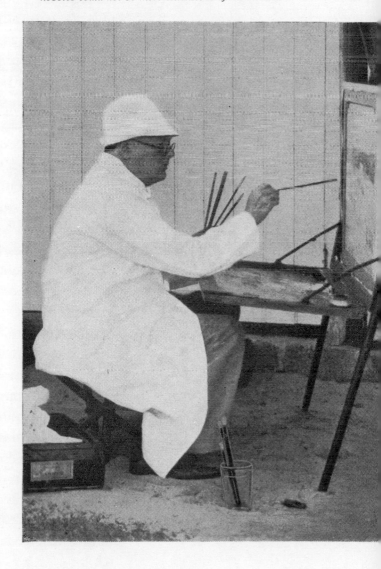

your friends, let them at any rate be your acquaintances. If they cannot enter the circle of your life, do not deny them at least a nod of recognition.

It is a mistake to read too many good books when quite young. A man once told me that he had read all the books that mattered. Cross-questioned, he appeared to have read a great many, but they seemed to have made only a slight impression. How many had he understood? How many had entered into his mental composition? How many had been hammered on the anvils of his mind, and afterwards ranged in an armoury of bright weapons ready to hand?

It is a great pity to read a book too soon in life. The first impression is the one that counts; and if it is a slight one, it may be all that can be hoped for. A later and second perusal may recoil from a surface already hardened by premature contact. Young people should be careful in their reading, as old people in eating their food. They should not eat too much. They should chew it well.

Since change is an essential element in diversion of all kinds, it is naturally more restful and refreshing to read in a different language from that in which one's ordinary daily work is done. To have a second language at your disposal, even if you only know it enough to read it with pleasure, is a sensible advantage. Our educationists are too often anxious to teach children so many different languages that they never get far enough in any one to derive any use or enjoyment from their study. The boy learns enough Latin to detest it; enough Greek to pass an examination; enough French to get from Calais to Paris; enough German to exhibit a diploma; enough Spanish or Italian to tell which is which; but not enough of any to secure the enormous boon of access to a second literature. Choose well, choose wisely, and choose one. Concentrate upon that one. Do not be content until you find yourself reading in it with real enjoyment. The process of reading for pleasure in another language rests the mental muscles; it enlivens the mind by a different sequence and emphasis of ideas. The mere form of speech excites the activity of separate brain-cells, relieving in the most effective manner the fatigue of those in hackneyed use. One may imagine that a man who blew the trumpet for his living would be glad to play the violin for his amusement. So it is with reading in another language than your own.

But reading and book-love in all their forms suffer from one serious defect: they are too nearly akin to the ordinary

Church by Lake Como, September, 1945

daily round of the brain-worker to give that element of change and contrast essential to real relief. To restore psychic equilibrium we should call into use those parts of the mind which direct both eye and hand. Many men have found great advantage in practising a handicraft for pleasure. Joinery, chemistry, book-binding, even brick-laying—if one were interested in them and skilful at them —would give a real relief to the over-tired brain. But, best of all and easiest to procure are sketching and painting in all their forms. I consider myself very lucky that late in life I have been able to develop this new taste and pastime. Painting came to my rescue in a most trying time, and I shall venture in the pages that follow to express the gratitude I feel.

By Lake Lugano, 1945

*The Mediterranean near Genoa,
September, 1945*

Near Antibes

68

*Lakeside Scene, Lake Como,
September, 1945*

St. Jean-Cap Ferrat

A Vase of Flowers

The Mill, Saint-Georges-Motel, Normandy

70

Painting is a companion with whom one may hope to walk a great part of life's journey,

'Age cannot wither her nor custom stale
Her infinite variety.'

One by one the more vigorous sports and exacting games fall away. Exceptional exertions are purchased only by a more pronounced and more prolonged fatigue. Muscles may relax, and feet and hands slow down; the nerve of youth and manhood may become less trusty. But painting is a friend who makes no undue demands, excites to no exhausting pursuits, keeps faithful pace even with feeble steps, and holds her canvas as a screen between us and the envious eyes of Time or the surly advance of Decrepitude.

Happy are the painters, for they shall not be lonely. Light and colour, peace and hope, will keep them company to the end, or almost to the end, of the day.

To have reached the age of forty without ever handling a brush or fiddling with a pencil, to have regarded with mature eye the painting of pictures of any kind as a mystery, to have stood agape before the chalk of the pavement artist, and then suddenly to find oneself plunged in the middle of a new and intense form of interest and action with paints and palettes and canvases, and not to be discouraged by results, is an astonishing and enriching experience. I hope it may be shared by others. I should be glad if these lines induced others to try the experiment which I have tried, and if some at least were to find themselves dowered with an absorbing new amusement delightful to themselves, and at any rate not violently harmful to man or beast.

I hope this is modest enough: because there is no subject on which I feel more humble or yet at the same time more natural. I do not presume to explain how to paint, but only how to get enjoyment. Do not turn the superior eye of critical passivity upon these efforts. Buy a paint-box and have a try. If you need something to occupy your leisure, to divert your mind from the daily round, to illuminate your holidays, do not be too ready to believe that you cannot find what you want here. Even at the advanced age of forty! It would be a sad pity to shuffle or scramble along through one's playtime with golf and bridge, pottering, loitering, shifting from one heel to the other, wondering what on earth to do—as perhaps is the fate of some unhappy beings—when all the while, if you only knew, there is close at hand a wonderful new world of thought and craft, a sunlit garden gleaming with light and colour of which you have the key in your waistcoat-pocket. Inexpensive independence, a mobile and perennial pleasure apparatus, new mental food and exercise, the old harmonies and symmetries in an entirely different language, an added interest to every common scene, an occupation for every idle hour, an unceasing voyage of entrancing discovery—these are high prizes. Make quite sure they are not yours. After all, if you try, and fail, there is not much harm done. The nursery will grab what the studio has rejected. And then you can always go out and kill some animal, humiliate some rival on the links, or despoil some friend across the green table. You will not be worse off in any way. In fact you will be better off. You will know 'beyond a peradventure,' to quote a phrase disagreeably reminiscent, that that is really what you were meant to do in your hours of relaxation.

But if, on the contrary, you are inclined—late in life though it be—to reconnoitre a foreign sphere of limitless extent, then be persuaded that the first quality that is needed is Audacity. There really is no time for the deliberate approach. Two years of drawing-lessons, three years of copying woodcuts, five years of plaster casts—these are for the young. They have enough to bear. And this thorough grounding is for those who, hearing the call in the morning of their days, are able to make painting their paramount lifelong vocation. The truth and beauty of line and form which by the slightest touch or twist of the brush a real artist imparts to every feature of his design must be founded on long, hard, persevering apprenticeship and a practice so habitual that it has become instinctive. We must not be too ambitious. We cannot aspire to masterpieces. We may content ourselves with a joy ride in a paint-box. And for this Audacity is the only ticket.

I shall now relate my personal experience. When I left the Admiralty at the end of May, 1915, I still remained a member of the Cabinet and of the War Council. In this position I knew everything and could do nothing. The change from the intense executive activities of each day's work at the Admiralty to the narrowly measured duties of a counsellor left me gasping. Like a sea-beast fished up from the depths, or a diver too suddenly hoisted, my

Marrakech, Morocco, around 1947

veins threatened to burst from the fall in pressure. I had great anxiety and no means of relieving it; I had vehement convictions and small power to give effect to them. I had to watch the unhappy casting-away of great opportunities, and the feeble execution of plans which I had launched and in which I heartily believed. I had long hours of utterly unwonted leisure in which to contemplate the frightful unfolding of the War. At a moment when every fibre of my being was inflamed to action, I was forced to remain a spectator of the tragedy, placed cruelly in a front seat. And then it was that the Muse of Painting came to my rescue—out of charity and out of chivalry, because after all she had nothing to do with me—and said, 'Are these toys any good to you? They amuse some people.'

Some experiments one Sunday in the country with the children's paint-box led me to procure the next morning a complete outfit for painting in oils.

Having bought the colours, an easel, and a canvas, the next step was *to begin*. But what a step to take! The palette gleamed with beads of colour; fair and white rose the canvas; the empty brush hung poised, heavy with destiny, irresolute in the air. My hand seemed arrested by a silent veto. But after all the sky on this occasion was unquestionably blue, and a pale blue at that. There could be no doubt that blue paint mixed with white should be put on the top part of the canvas. One really does not need to have had an artist's training to see that. It is a starting-point open to all. So very gingerly I mixed a little blue paint on the palette with a very small brush, and then with infinite precaution made a mark about as big as a bean upon the affronted snow-white shield. It was a challenge, a deliberate challenge; but so subdued, so halting, indeed so cataleptic, that it deserved no response. At that moment the loud approaching sound of a motor-car was heard in the drive. From this chariot there stepped swiftly and lightly none other than the gifted wife of Sir John Lavery. 'Painting! But what are you hesitating about? Let me have a brush—the big one.' Splash into the turpentine, wallop into the blue and the white, frantic flourish on the palette—clean no longer—and then several large, fierce strokes and slashes of blue on the absolutely cowering canvas. Anyone could see that it could not hit back. No evil fate avenged the jaunty violence. The canvas grinned in helplessness before me. The spell was broken. The sickly inhibitions rolled away. I seized the largest

Flowers, painted in the studio at Chartwell

brush and fell upon my victim with Berserk fury. I have never felt any awe of a canvas since.

Everyone knows the feelings with which one stands shivering on a spring-board, the shock when a friendly foe steals up behind and hurls you into the flood, and the ardent glow which thrills you as you emerge breathless from the plunge.

This beginning with Audacity, or being thrown into the middle of it, is already a very great part of the art of painting. But there is more in it than that.

> '*La peinture à l'huile*
> *Est bien difficile,*
> *Mais c'est beaucoup plus beau*
> *Que la peinture à l'eau.*'

Orchids

I write no word in disparagement of water-colours. But there really is nothing like oils. You have a medium at your disposal which offers real power, if you only can find out how to use it. Moreover, it is easier to get a certain distance along the road by its means than by water-colour. First of all, you can correct mistakes much more easily. One sweep of the palette-knife 'lifts' the blood and tears of a morning from the canvas and enables a fresh start to be made; indeed the canvas is all the better for past impressions. Secondly, you can approach your problem from any direction. You need not build downwards awkwardly from white paper to your darkest dark. You may strike where you please, beginning if you will with a moderate central arrangement of middle tones, and then hurling in the extremes when the psychological moment comes. Lastly, the pigment itself is such nice stuff to handle (if it does not retaliate). You can build it on layer after layer if you like. You can keep on experimenting. You can change your plan to meet the exigencies of time or weather. And always remember you can scrape it all away.

Just to paint is great fun. The colours are lovely to look at and delicious to squeeze out. Matching them, however crudely, with what you see is fascinating and absolutely absorbing. Try it if you have not done so—before you die. As one slowly begins to escape from the difficulties of

choosing the right colours and laying them on in the right places and in the right way, wider considerations come into view. One begins to see, for instance, that painting a picture is like fighting a battle; and trying to paint a picture is, I suppose, like trying to fight a battle. It is, if anything, more exciting than fighting it successfully. But the principle is the same. It is the same kind of problem as unfolding a long, sustained, interlocked argument. It is a proposition which, whether of few or numberless parts, is commanded by a single unity of conception. And we think—though I cannot tell—that painting a great picture must require an intellect on the grand scale. There must be that all-embracing view which presents the beginning and the end, the whole and each part, as one instantaneous impression retentively and untiringly held in the mind. When we look at the larger Turners—canvases yards wide and tall—and observe that they are all done in one piece and represent one single second of time, and that every innumerable detail, however small, however distant, however subordinate, is set forth naturally and in its true proportion and relation, without effort, without failure, we must feel in the presence of an intellectual manifestation the equal in quality and intensity of the finest achievements of warlike action, of forensic argument, or of scientific or philosophical adjudication.

The Goldfish Pool at Chartwell, in the garden of Mr. Churchill's Kent home. Exhibited at the Royal Academy, 1948

In all battles two things are usually required of the Commander-in-Chief: to make a good plan for his army and, secondly, to keep a strong reserve. Both these are also obligatory upon the painter. To make a plan, thorough reconnaissance of the country where the battle is to be fought is needed. Its fields, its mountains, its rivers, its bridges, its trees, its flowers, its atmosphere—all require and repay attentive observation from a special point of view. One is quite astonished to find how many things there are in the landscape, and in every object in it, one never noticed before. And this is a tremendous new pleasure and interest which invests every walk or drive with an added object. So many colours on the hillside, each different in shadow and in sunlight; such brilliant reflections in the pool, each a key lower than what they repeat; such lovely lights gilding or silvering surface or outline, all tinted exquisitely with pale colour, rose, orange, green, or violet. I found myself instinctively as I walked noting the tint and character of a leaf, the dreamy, purple shades of mountains, the exquisite lacery of winter branches, the dim, pale silhouettes of far horizons. And I had lived for over forty years without ever noticing any of them except in a general way, as one might look at a crowd and say, 'What a lot of people!'

I think this heightened sense of observation of Nature is one of the chief delights that have come to me through trying to paint. No doubt many people who are lovers of art have acquired it in a high degree without actually practising. But I expect that nothing will make one observe more quickly or more thoroughly than having to face the difficulty of representing the thing observed. And mind you, if you do observe accurately and with refinement, and if you do record what you have seen with tolerable correspondence, the result follows on the canvas with startling obedience. Even if only four or five main features are seized and truly recorded, these by themselves will carry a lot of ill-success or half-success. Answer five big questions out of all the hundreds in the examination paper correctly and well, and though you may not win a prize, at any rate you will not be absolutely ploughed.

But in order to make his plan, the General must not only reconnoitre the battle-ground, he must also study the achievements of the great Captains of the past. He must bring the observations he has collected in the field into comparison with the treatment of similar incidents by famous chiefs. Then the galleries of Europe take on a new —and to me at least a severely practical—interest. 'This, then, is how —— painted a cataract. Exactly, and there is that same light I noticed last week in the waterfall at ——.' And so on. You see the difficulty that baffled you yesterday; and you see how easily it has been overcome by a great or even by a skilful painter. Not only is your observation of Nature sensibly improved and developed, but you look at the masterpieces of art with an analysing and a comprehending eye.

The whole world is open with all its treasures. The simplest objects have their beauty. Every garden presents innumerable fascinating problems. Every land, every parish, has its own tale to tell. And there are many lands differing from each other in countless ways, and each presenting delicious variants of colour, light, form, and definition. Obviously, then, armed with a paint-box, one cannot be bored, one cannot be left at a loose end, one cannot 'have several days on one's hands.' Good gracious! what there is to admire and how little time there is to see it in! For the first time one begins to envy Methuselah. No doubt he made a very indifferent use of his opportunities.

But it is in the use and withholding of their reserves that the great Commanders have generally excelled. After all, when once the last reserve has been thrown in, the Commander's part is played. If that does not win the battle, he has nothing else to give. The event must be left to luck

Village near Lugano, September, 1945

The Tapestries at Blenheim Palace.
Exhibited at the Royal Academy, 1948

Olive grove, La Dragonière,
near Monte Carlo

and to the fighting troops. But these last, in the absence of high direction, are apt to get into sad confusion, all mixed together in a nasty mess, without order or plan— and consequently without effect. Mere masses count no more. The largest brush, the brightest colours, cannot even make an impression. The pictorial battlefield becomes a sea of mud mercifully veiled by the fog of war. It is evident there has been a serious defeat. Even though the General plunges in himself and emerges bespattered, as he sometimes does, he will not retrieve the day.

In painting, the reserves consist in Proportion or Relation. And it is here that the art of the painter marches along the road which is traversed by all the greatest harmonies in thought. At one side of the palette there is white, at the other black; and neither is ever used 'neat.' Between these two rigid limits all the action must lie, all the power required must be generated. Black and white themselves, placed in juxtaposition, make no great impression; and yet they are the most that you can do in pure contrast. It is wonderful—after one has tried and failed often—to see how easily and surely the true artist is able to produce every effect of light and shade, of sunshine and shadow, of distance or nearness, simply by expressing justly the relations between the different planes and surfaces with which he is dealing. We think that this is founded upon a sense of proportion, trained no doubt by practice, but which in its essence is a frigid manifestation of mental power and size. We think that the same mind's eye that can justly survey and appraise and prescribe beforehand the values of a truly great picture in one all-embracing regard, in one flash of simultaneous and homogeneous comprehension, would also with a certain acquaintance with the special technique be able to pronounce with sureness upon any other high activity of the human intellect. This was certainly true of the great Italians.

I have written in this way to show how varied are the delights which may be gained by those who enter hopefully and thoughtfully upon the pathway of painting; how enriched they will be in their daily vision, how fortified in their independence, how happy in their leisure. Whether you feel that your soul is pleased by the conception or contemplation of harmonies, or that your mind is stimulated by the aspect of magnificent problems, or whether you are content to find fun in trying to observe and depict the jolly things you see, the vistas of possibility are limited only by the shortness of life. Every day you may make progress. Every step may be fruitful. Yet there will stretch out before you an ever-lengthening, ever-ascending, ever-improving path. You know you will never get to the end of the journey. But this, so far from discouraging, only adds to the joy and glory of the climb.

Try it, then, before it is too late and before you mock at me. Try it while there is time to overcome the preliminary difficulties. Learn enough of the language in your prime to open this new literature to your age. Plant a garden in which you can sit when digging days are done. It may be only a small garden, but you will see it grow. Year by year it will bloom and ripen. Year by year it will be better cultivated. The weeds will be cast out. The fruit-trees will be pruned and trained. The flowers will bloom in more beautiful combinations. There will be sunshine there even in the winter-time, and cool shade, and the play of shadow on the pathway in the shining days of June.

I must say I like bright colours. I agree with Ruskin in his denunciation of that school of painting who 'eat slate-pencil and chalk, and assure everybody that they are nicer and purer than strawberries and plums.' I cannot pretend to feel impartial about the colours. I rejoice with the brilliant ones, and am genuinely sorry for the poor browns. When I get to heaven I mean to spend a considerable portion of my first million years in painting, and so get to the bottom of the subject. But then I shall require a still gayer palette than I get here below. I expect orange and vermilion will be the darkest, dullest colours upon it, and beyond them there will be a whole range of wonderful new colours which will delight the celestial eye.

Chance led me one autumn to a secluded nook on the Côte d'Azur, between Marseilles and Toulon, and there I fell in with one or two painters who revelled in the methods of the modern French school. These were disciples of Cézanne. They view Nature as a mass of shimmering light in which forms and surfaces are comparatively unimportant, indeed hardly visible, but which gleams and glows with beautiful harmonies and contrasts of colour. Certainly it was of great interest to me to come suddenly in contact with this entirely different way of looking at things. I had hitherto painted the sea flat, with long, smooth strokes of mixed pigment in which the tints

Chartwell under Snow. Exhibited at the Royal Academy, 1947

varied only by gradations. Now I must try to represent it by innumerable small separate lozenge-shaped points and patches of colour—often pure colour—so that it looked more like a tessellated pavement than a marine picture. It sounds curious. All the same, do not be in a hurry to reject the method. Go back a few yards and survey the result. Each of these little points of colour is now playing his part in the general effect. Individually invisible, he sets up a strong radiation, of which the eye is conscious without detecting the cause. Look also at the blue of the Mediterranean. How can you depict and record it? Certainly not by any single colour that was ever manufactured. The only way in which that luminous intensity of blue can be simulated is by this multitude of tiny points of varied colour all in true relation to the rest of the scheme. Difficult? Fascinating!

Nature presents itself to the eye through the agency of these individual points of light, each of which sets up the vibrations peculiar to its colour. The brilliancy of a picture must therefore depend partly upon the frequency with which these points are found on any given area of the canvas, and partly on their just relation to one another. Ruskin says in his *Elements of Drawing,* from which I have already quoted, 'You will not, in Turner's largest oil pictures, perhaps six or seven feet long by four or five high, find one spot of colour as large as a grain of wheat ungradated.' But the gradations of Turner differ from those of the modern French school by being gently and almost imperceptibly evolved one from another instead of being bodily and even roughly separated; and the brush of Turner followed the form of the objects he depicted, while our French friends often seem to take a pride in directly opposing it. For instance, they would prefer to paint a sea with up and down strokes rather than with horizontal; or a tree-trunk from right to left rather than up and down. This, I expect, is due to falling in love with one's theories, and making sacrifices of truth to them in order to demonstrate fidelity and admiration.

But surely we owe a debt to those who have so wonderfully vivified, brightened, and illuminated modern landscape painting. Have not Manet and Monet, Cézanne and Matisse, rendered to painting something of the same service which Keats and Shelley gave to poetry after the solemn and ceremonious literary perfections of the eighteenth century? They have brought back to the pictorial art a new draught of *joie de vivre*; and the beauty of their work is instinct with gaiety, and floats in sparkling air.

I do not expect these masters would particularly appreciate my defence, but I must avow an increasing attraction to their work. Lucid and exact expression is one of the characteristics of the French mind. The French language has been made the instrument of the admirable gift. Frenchmen talk and write just as well about painting as they have done about love, about war, about diplomacy, or cooking. Their terminology is precise and complete. They are therefore admirably equipped to be teachers in the theory of any of these arts. Their critical faculty is so powerfully developed that it is perhaps some restraint upon achievement. But it is a wonderful corrective to others as well as to themselves.

My French friend, for instance, after looking at some of my daubs, took me round the galleries of Paris, pausing here and there. Wherever he paused, I found myself before a picture which I particularly admired. He then explained that it was quite easy to tell, from the kind of things I had been trying to do, what were the things I liked. Never having taken any interest in pictures till I tried to paint, I had no preconceived opinions. I just felt, for reasons I could not fathom, that I liked some much more than others. I was astonished that anyone else should, on the most cursory observation of my work, be able so surely to divine a taste which I had never consciously formed. My friend said that it is not a bad thing

Venice, 1951

The Loup River, Quebec. Exhibited at the Royal Academy, 1947

to know nothing at all about pictures, but to have a matured mind trained in other things and a new strong interest for painting. The elements are there from which a true taste in art can be formed with time and guidance, and there are no obstacles or imperfect conceptions in the way. I hope this is true. Certainly the last part is true.

Once you begin to study it, all Nature is equally interesting and equally charged with beauty. I was shown a picture by Cézanne of a blank wall of a house, which he had made instinct with the most delicate lights and colours. Now I often amuse myself when I am looking at a wall or a flat surface of any kind by trying to distinguish all the different colours and tints which can be discerned upon it, and considering whether these arise from reflections or from natural hue. You would be astonished the first time you tried this to see how many and what beautiful colours there are even in the most commonplace objects, and the more carefully and frequently you look the more variations do you perceive.

But these are no reasons for limiting oneself to the plainest and most ordinary objects and scenes. Mere prettiness of scene, to be sure, is not needed for a beautiful picture. In fact, artificially-made pretty places are very often a hindrance to a good picture. Nature will hardly stand a double process of beautification: one layer of idealism on top of another is too much of a good thing. But a vivid scene, a brilliant atmosphere, novel and charming lights, impressive contrasts, if they strike the eye all at once, arouse an interest and an ardour which will certainly be reflected in the work which you try to do, and will make it seem easier.

It would be interesting if some real authority investigated carefully the part which memory plays in painting. We look at the object with an intent regard, then at the palette, and thirdly at the canvas. The canvas receives a message dispatched usually a few seconds before from the natural object. But it has come through a post-office *en route*. It has been transmitted in code. It has been turned from light into paint. It reaches the canvas a cryptogram. Not until it has been placed in its correct relation to everything else that is on the canvas can it be deciphered, is its meaning apparent, is it translated once again from mere pigment into light. And the light this time is not of Nature but of Art. The whole of this considerable process is carried through on the wings or the wheels of memory.

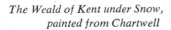

The Weald of Kent under Snow, painted from Chartwell

In most cases we think it is the wings—airy and quick like a butterfly from flower to flower. But all heavy traffic and all that has to go a long journey must travel on wheels.

In painting in the open air the sequence of actions is so rapid that the process of translation into and out of pigment may seem to be unconscious. But all the greatest landscapes have been painted indoors, and often long after the first impressions were gathered. In a dim cellar the Dutch or Italian master recreated the gleaming ice of a Netherlands carnival or the lustrous sunshine of Venice or the Campagna. Here, then, is required a formidable memory of the visual kind. Not only do we develop our powers of observation, but also those of carrying the record—of carrying it through an extraneous medium and of reproducing it, hours, days, or even months after the scene has vanished or the sunlight died.

I was told by a friend that when Whistler guided a school in Paris he made his pupils observe their model on the ground floor, and then run upstairs and paint their picture piece by piece on the floor above. As they became more proficient, he put their easels up a storey higher, till at last the *élite* were scampering with their decision up six flights into the attic—praying it would not evaporate on the way. This is, perhaps, only a tale. But it shows effectively of what enormous importance a trained, accurate, retentive memory must be to an artist; and conversely what a useful exercise painting may be for the development of an accurate and retentive memory.

There is no better exercise for the would-be artist than to study and devour a picture, and then, without looking at it again, to attempt the next day to reproduce it. Nothing can more exactly measure the progress both of observation and memory. It is still harder to compose out of many separate, well-retained impressions, aided though they be by sketches and colour notes, a new, complete conception. But this is the only way in which great landscapes have been painted—or can be painted. The size of the canvas alone precludes its being handled out of doors. The fleeting light imposes a rigid time-limit. The same light never returns. One cannot go back day after day without the picture getting stale. The painter must choose between a rapid impression, fresh and warm and living, but probably deserving only of a short life, and the cold, profound, intense effort of memory, knowledge, and will-power, prolonged perhaps for weeks, from which a masterpiece can alone result. It is much better not to fret too much about the latter. Leave to the masters of art trained by a lifetime of devotion the wonderful process of picture-building and picture-creation. Go out into the sunlight and be happy with what you see.

Painting is complete as a distraction. I know of nothing which, without exhausting the body, more entirely absorbs the mind. Whatever the worries of the hour or the threats of the future, once the picture has begun to flow along, there is no room for them in the mental screen. They pass out into shadow and darkness. All one's mental light, such as it is, becomes concentrated on the task. Time stands respectfully aside, and it is only after many hesitations that luncheon knocks gruffly at the door. When I have had to stand up on parade, or even, I regret to say, in church, for half an hour at a time, I have always felt that the erect position is not natural to man, has only been painfully acquired, and is only with fatigue and

The Blue Room, Trent Park, the home of the late Sir Phillip Sassoon. Exhibited at the Royal Academy, 1948

difficulty maintained. But no one who is fond of painting finds the slightest inconvenience, as long as the interest holds, in standing to paint for three or four hours at a stretch.

Lastly, let me say a word on painting as a spur to travel. There is really nothing like it. Every day and all day is provided with its expedition and its occupation—cheap, attainable, innocent, absorbing, recuperative. The vain racket of the tourist gives place to the calm enjoyment of the philosopher, intensified by an enthralling sense of action and endeavour. Every country where the sun shines and every district in it, has a theme of its own. The lights, the atmosphere, the aspect, the spirit, are all different; but each has its native charm. Even if you are only a poor painter you can feel the influence of the scene, guiding your brush, selecting the tubes you squeeze on to the palette. Even if you cannot portray it as you see it, you feel it, you know it, and you admire it for ever. When people rush about Europe in the train from one glittering centre of work or pleasure to another, passing—at enormous expense—through a series of mammoth hotels and blatant carnivals, they little know what they are missing, and how cheaply priceless things can be obtained. The painter wanders and loiters contentedly from place to place, always on the look out for some brilliant butterfly of a picture which can be caught and set up and carried safely home.

Now I am learning to like painting even on dull days. But in my hot youth I demanded sunshine. Sir William Orpen advised me to visit Avignon on account of its wonderful light, and certainly there is no more delightful centre for a would-be painter's activities: then Egypt, fierce and brilliant, presenting in infinite variety the single triplex theme of the Nile, the desert, and the sun; or Palestine, a land of rare beauty—the beauty of the turquoise and the opal—which well deserves the attention of some real artist, and has never been portrayed to the extent that is its due. And what of India? Who has ever interpreted its lurid splendours? But after all, if only the sun will shine, one does not need to go beyond one's own country. There is nothing more intense than the burnished steel and gold of a Highland stream; and at the beginning and close of almost every day the Thames displays to the citizens of London glories and delights which one must travel far to rival.

St. Jean-Cap Ferrat, Mediterranean resort, near Monaco, 1946

Historic 10 Downing Street, official residence of Britain's Prime Minister, was occupied by Churchill during two separate periods as the nation's most powerful political leader.

EPILOGUE

Tributes

When there was darkness in the world and hope was low in the hearts of men, a generous Providence gave us Winston Churchill. As long as men tell of that time of terrible danger and of the men who won the victory, the name of Churchill will live. Let us give thanks that we knew him. With our grief let there be gratitude for a life so fully lived, for service so splendid, and for the joy he gave by the joy he took in all he did. The people of the United States—his cousins and fellow citizens—will pray with his British countrymen for God's eternal blessing on this man, and for comfort to his family. He is history's child, and what he said and what he did will never die.

President Lyndon B. Johnson (U.S.)

Democracy has lost one of its greatest champions. With his death an era has come to an end. But he will live in the hearts of the American people just as Lincoln, Jackson, Franklin Roosevelt and John F. Kennedy.

Vice President Hubert H. Humphrey (U.S.)

The whole world is the poorer by the loss of his many-sided genius. While the survival of this country and the sister nations of the Commonwealth in the face of the greatest danger that has ever threatened them will be a perpetual memorial to his leadership, his vision and his indomitable courage.

Queen Elizabeth II (U.K.)

He will be mourned all over the world by all who owe so much to him. He is now at peace after a life in which he created history and it will be remembered as long as history is read.

Prime Minister Harold Wilson (U.K.)

He was the greatest of war leaders, but it was his deep and spontaneous humanity which drew the response of millions who did not know him but felt instinctively that he was their friend.

Former Prime Minister Sir Alec Douglas-Home (U.K.)

He has handed on to his successors this passionate belief that freedom, perhaps even the survival, of the civilized world depends on the closest association between the two branches of the English-Speaking peoples.

Former Prime Minister Harold Macmillan (U.K.)

Please accept the Soviet Government's and my own personal condolences on the passing of Sir Winston Churchill, outstanding British statesman. The tireless efforts of Sir Winston during the war against Hitlerite Germany are remembered in the Soviet Union and the grief of the British people in this bereavement is shared here.

Premier Aleksei N. Kosygin (U.S.S.R.)

For everyone in my country as for myself, Sir Winston Churchill is and will remain the one who—in directing the admirable British war effort to victory—contributed powerfully to the well-being of the French people and the liberty of the world.

President Charles De Gaulle (France)

The glory which surrounded him in life will continue to shine from him even after death and so long as there is a free man on this earth his name will be remembered with gratitude.

President Giuseppe Saragat (Italy)

I feel with you and your family the grief which afflicts you on the death of this truly great man, who united in himself in a remarkable way real humanity with political range of vision and energy of genius.

Former Chancellor Konrad Adenauer (West Germany)

Winston Churchill's mortal remains have passed on, but his spirit will live on for centuries. He typified man's resolution to be free and man's courage to face and overcome those who would threaten his liberties and free institutions.

Former President Harry S. Truman (U.S.)

The Churchill catafalque in St. Paul's Cathedral is surrounded by mourners from all nations during the funeral service.

CHURCHILL

When in the evening
The black wash came round the island
In an evil flood,
And many voices cried:
"Why do we stand? What out of all
Is secure?
What work is not worn down,
Is not made sand?"
Then your voice spoke
Out of the heart of another century
Reiterating England.

There in darkness,
There in a wash of lies
That eats like acid at the feet of men,
When men said to each other
"There is no answer,"
You spoke for Trafalgar
And for the sombre lions in the square.

Maxwell Anderson

We share your sorrow and feel greatly the loss of the man who has been such an inspiration to all free people of the world. He characterized to all Americans the closeness of the ties between our two countries.

Secretary of State Dean Rusk (U.S.)

The lasting tribute we can pay him is to continue to work for the principles of peace and democracy for which he lived and fought all his life.

Prime Minister Lal Bahadur Shastri (India)

One measure of Churchill's greatness is that no one today, now that the blaze of his genius has subsided into dust and ashes, need explain or describe or grope for words. He is one of those rare figures in history who stand like skyscrapers above the merely great. Usually history waits to recognize its supreme leaders, but there is no need to wait in Churchill's case. . . .

A man like Winston Churchill makes everyone a part of his life, as if a little of that greatness were shared by each of us.

The New York Times (U.S.)

Today we meet in sadness to mourn one of the world's greatest citizens. Sir Winston Churchill is dead. The voice that led nations, raised armies, inspired victories, and blew fresh courage into the hearts of men is silenced. We shall hear no longer the remembered eloquence and wit, the old courage and defiance, the robust serenity of indomitable faith. Our world is thus poorer, our political dialogue is diminished, and the sources of public inspiration run more thinly for all of us. There is "a lonesome place against the sky." . . .

Contemplating this completed career, we feel a sense of enlargement and exhilaration. Like the grandeur and power of the masterpieces of art and music, Churchill's life uplifts our hearts and fills us with fresh revelation of the scale and reach of human achievement. We may be sad; but we rejoice as well, as all must rejoice when they "now praise famous men" and see in their lives the full splendor of our human estate.

He used to say that he was half American and all English. But we put that right when the Congress made him an honorary citizen of his mother's native land and we shall always claim a part of him. I remember once years ago during a long visit at his country house he talked proudly of his American Revolutionary ancestors and happily of his boyhood visits to the United States. As I took my leave I said

I was going back to London to speak to the English-Speaking Union and asked if he had any message for them. "Yes," he said, "tell them that you bring greetings from an English-Speaking Union." And I think that perhaps it was to the relations of the United Kingdom and the United States that he made his finest contribution.

Ambassador Adlai E. Stevenson (U.S.)

Upon the Mighty Thames, a great avenue of history, move at this moment to their final resting place the mortal remains of Sir Winston Churchill. He was a great maker of history, but his work done, the record closed, we can almost hear him, with the poet [Tennyson], say:

Sunset and evening star,
And one clear call for me!

Twilight and evening bell,
And after that the dark!
And may there be no sadness
  of farewell,
When I embark.

As I, like all other free men, pause to pay a personal tribute to the giant who now passes from among us, I have no charter to speak for my countrymen—only for myself. But, if in memory, we journey back two decades to the time when America and Britain stood shoulder to shoulder in global conflict against tyranny, then I can presume—with propriety, I think—to act as spokesman for the millions of Americans who served with me and with their British comrades during those three years of war on this sector of the earth.

To those men Winston Churchill *was* Britain—he was the embodiment of British defiance to threat, her courage in adversity, her calmness in danger, her moderation in success. Among the Allies his name was spoken with respect, admiration and affection. Although they loved to chuckle at his foibles, they knew he was a staunch friend. They felt his inspirational leadership. They counted him a fighter in their ranks.

The loyalty that the fighting forces of many nations here serving gave to him during the war was no less strong, nor less freely given, than he had, in such full measure, from his own countrymen.

An American, I was one of those Allies. During those dramatic months I was privileged to meet, to talk, to plan and to work with him for common goals.

Out of that association an abiding—and to me precious—friendship was forged; it withstood the trials and frictions inescapable among men of strong convictions living, in the atmosphere of war.

The war ended, our friendship flowered in the later and more subtle tests imposed by international politics. Then, each of us, holding high official posts in his own nation, strove together so to concert the strength of our two peoples that liberty might be preserved among men and the security of the free world wholly sustained.

Through a career during which personal victories alternated with defeats, glittering praise with bitter criticism, intense public activity with periods of semi-retirement, Winston Churchill lived out his four score and ten years.

With no thought of the length of the time he might be permitted on earth, he was concerned only with the quality of the service he could render to his nation and to humanity. Though he had no fear of death, he coveted always the opportunity to continue that service.

At this moment, as our hearts stand at attention, we say our affectionate, though sad, goodby to the leader to whom the entire body of free men owes so much.

In the coming years, many in countless words will strive to interpret the motives, describe the accomplishments and extol the virtues of Winston Churchill—soldier, statesman and citizen that two great countries were proud to claim as their own. Among all the things so written or spoken, there will ring out through all the centuries one incontestable refrain: Here was a champion of freedom.

May God grant that we—and the generations who will remember him—heed the lessons he taught us: in his deeds, in his words, in his life.

May we carry on his work until no nation lies in captivity; no man is denied opportunity for fulfillment.

And now to you, Sir Winston—my old friend—farewell!

Former President Dwight D. Eisenhower (U.S.)

I, and the people of Ghana, pray that the sun will shine gently on Lady Churchill, on her family and on all who were near and dear to Sir Winston.

President Kwame Nkrumah (Ghana)

He was a politician of complete integrity and independence, honesty, candor and courage, a prolific writer of considerable lucidity and eloquence, a gallant soldier of great imagination. He was above all a great man.

Prime Minister Jomo Kenyatta (Kenya)

We share the great sorrow of the British nation.

Prime Minister Hendrik F. Verwoerd (South Africa)

We at the United Nations feel a particular grief at the death of one who played such a vital role in the formation of our organization, from its conception in the Atlantic Charter to its realization in San Francisco. This achievement takes its place alongside countless others and together with his inspiring leadership and his own late historical works will always remain as a memorial to him.

U Thant (Secretary General of the U.N.)

A giant has gone out from among us. We are all poorer for his going. I have lost a cherished friend, Britain has lost her most luminous son, free men everywhere have lost their champion.

Bernard Baruch

Please accept the expression of profound sympathy of the people of Cyprus, my Government and myself on the loss of your beloved husband, the great man who now belongs to the ages.

Archbishop Makarios (Cyprus)

The world has lost a great statesman, not only of our century but of all time. Turkey shares the sorrow of the English nation.

Premier Ismet Inonu (Turkey)

Above all, Sir Winston will go down in history as one who personified by word and deed the deep yearnings of mankind for freedom.

Prince Abdul Rahman (Malaysia)

He dies sure of his majestic place in history, and leaves to his countrymen a name inseparable from their proudest and bravest memories.

The Times (U.K.)

He drew strength from the unconquerable will of the British people, and they drew strength from him.

The Sun (U.K.)

He was the voice of Britain, and though he deprecatingly said that he had been privileged to "give the roar," his speeches were worth an army.

The Scotsman (U.K.)

If one word can sum up his career, it is magnanimity—greatness in combat and also greatness in tolerance and reconciliation.

The Manchester Guardian (U.K.)

If men—and not in Britain alone—enjoy liberty, if they live without shame, if they can indulge the hope of building a better world, then it is to this man above all men that they owe their priceless blessings.

The Daily Express (U.K.)

It has been said that England always finds the right man in her hour of peril. If the man matches the peril, then truly can it be said that this country has never known so great a man as Winston Churchill.

The Daily Mail (U.K.)

Churchill's tale is already written in history, not of his nation alone but in our history too, and Germany's, and Russia's and the world's. To say that Churchill saved Western civilization is to say too much, but Western civilization without him would have had a harder time saving itself.

The Baltimore Sun (U.S.)

He defied the theory of historical necessity that says man is shaped by his times. He put his own mark on the world.

The Chicago Sun-Times (U.S.)

As a domestic politician (in the best sense of the word) he may have had his weaknesses. As a military strategist he may have made his mistakes. As a statesman, responsible for the formulation of international policies, he may not have been infallible. As a leader of free men in a time of supreme crisis, Churchill was almost—if not—incomparable.

The Kansas City Star (U.S.)

Overleaf: The body of Winston Churchill lies in state in the somber stillness of Westminster Hall.

Freelance Photographers Guild

Gray coated Grenadier Guards place the Union Jack draped Churchill coffin on a caisson outside St. Paul's Cathedral.